English
Fairy Tales and
Legends

English
Fairy Tales and
Legends

ROSALIND KERVEN

National Trust

For Sue Mason

First published in Great Britain in 2008 by

National Trust Books
10 Southcombe Street
London W14 0RA

An imprint of Anova Books Ltd

ISBN 978 19054 0065 2

A CIP catalogue record for this book is available from the British Library.

16 15 14 13 12 11 10
10 9 8 7 6 5 4 3

Reproduction by Mission Productions Ltd, Hong Kong
Printed and bound by 1010 Printing International Ltd, China

This book can be ordered direct from the publisher at the website www.anovabooks.com, from your local bookshop and National Trust shops.

Contents

Introduction

An English childhood is peppered with fairy tales, yet surprisingly the
most familiar stories – Cinderella, Snow White, Aladdin and so on – are
not home-grown at all, but have their roots in France, Germany and the
Middle East. Does England not have its own store of tales? Of course it
does! And though most have, curiously, failed to find their way into the
popular collections, they are equally magical, amusing, haunting and,
indeed, astonishing.

Countless long-dead voices lie behind this rich cultural heritage, for
every fairy tale and legend has been developed and refined by successive
generations of anonymous authors. Traditional stories 'belong to
everyone', thus permitting each reteller to add a bit here, tweak something
there, colour it with his or her own personality or add a quaint snippet of
local flavour. Often the same story exists in several different versions,
either nationally or in different parts of the country.

In the manner of fairy tales and legends everywhere, the traditional
stories of England are set in a parallel world: fantastical, often illogical,
outside normal time and beyond the edges of reality, imbued with
supernatural elements and a dream-like quality. Typically, their plots
centre on a problem or challenge, and their dramatis personae are
anonymous ideal types ('a king', 'a peasant boy', 'a wise woman'), with
generous helpings of supernatural beings such as fairies, giants and
dragons. The stories tend towards an optimistic moral structure, with

justice fairly done, wickedness punished and goodness rewarded. However, they are stubbornly politically incorrect, portraying characters as old-fashioned stereotypes, offering no excuses for evil, and not flinching from the gruesome ends suffered by villains. Displaying weak, oppressed characters overcoming more powerful ones, and exploring major emotional issues, such as parental rejection and the need to 'prove' oneself, they have natural appeal to children. Yet they cannot be classified as children's stories, for they have the special quality of being able to entertain and uplift readers of *all* ages.

The stories were originally narrated aloud 'around the fireside', but the nineteenth century saw a golden age for folklore, when collectors all over the world began to gather these ancient tales from oral sources and write them down. In England (and indeed, in the rest of the United Kingdom and Ireland), such collections were made, often several times over, in every county. From these, anthologists put together their own country-wide selections, including the once much-loved *English Fairy Tales* (1890) and *More English Fairy Tales* (1894) by Joseph Jacobs, which included interesting annotations. This work was continued well into the twentieth century, culminating in the 1970s with Katherine M. Briggs's four-volume work, *A Dictionary of British Folk-Tales and Legends*. I am deeply indebted to this monumental collection, which reproduces stories from all over the country in their original forms, often in dialect. It was the most comprehensive and invaluable of the many sourcebooks I used to compile my own retellings.

But good stories need no further introduction. So leave the real world behind you for a while and forget your troubles as you enter the wildly irrational yet totally enchanting world of *English Fairy Tales and Legends*.

Rosalind Kerven
Northumberland, 2008

King Arthur and the Hideous Hag

· Cumbria ·

King Arthur and the Hideous Hag

 n the golden days when the Great Forest still spread across the land, and travellers could pass freely between this world and the faerie realms, good King Arthur had his court at Carlisle.

One New Year's Day, the king and all his knights were sitting at the Round Table making merry, when suddenly there was a frenzied knocking at the door. The next moment, a pretty farm girl came rushing in with her hair all tangled and her dress torn, weeping most piteously.

'Your majesty,' she cried, 'I beg you to help me!'

King Arthur rose to his feet at once. 'Fair lady,' he answered her courteously, 'I will be honoured to help you. But what troubles you?'

'An evil ogre has moved into Hewin Castle, sir!' wept the farm girl, wringing her hands. 'You know – the old fortress that stands on the fells above Wadlyn Tarn. I live on the opposite shore, and the ogre has been snatching girls and women from all the farms around there, and taking them up to his lair. Not one has ever come back. *Please*, your majesty, I beg you to send one of your knights to kill him!'

A murmur rippled through the bold company at the Round Table.

King Arthur said: 'The first adventure of this New Year! It must be mine! *I* will go to this evil ogre's castle and I shall destroy him single-handed.'

The king put on his armour and took up Excalibur, the wondrous sword that was forged in Faeryland and gifted him by the Lady of the Lake.

Then he mounted a white horse and rode with all speed, over the snow-topped fells and through the dark forest, until he reached the looming fortress of Hewin Castle. The sky was dark with storm clouds. King Arthur jumped from his mount, drew Excalibur and rapped upon the gates, calling:

'Show yourself, ogre! I am Arthur, High King of all this land. I order you to cease your evil – or else come out and fight me to the death.'

An ugly roar of laughter answered him. Then the castle door burst open and a huge, fearsome fellow came stooping through it. He was twice as tall as an ordinary man, with arms like great oak branches and a leering, slavering face.

'Why are you bothering me, Arthur?' the ogre spat. 'Who do you think you are, calling yourself "High King" and ordering me about like a common servant? Yes, I can see that pathetic piece of metal you're clutching and I've heard all about how mighty you're supposed to be. But, let me tell you this: *my* power comes from witchcraft and devilry, and it's far more dangerous than Excalibur. Just in case you don't believe me, I'll give you a taste of it.'

Arthur brandished his sword and made ready to run at the ogre. But before he could move, the ogre raised his left hand high above his head, sending a dazzle of lightning across the winter sky. King Arthur gave a strangled cry. He swayed and stumbled back. Excalibur slipped from his hand and his fingers clutched helplessly at the air. He began to shiver and tremble, his legs buckled and he fell to the ground.

'You viper!' he shouted. 'What have you done to me?' His voice was hoarse and cracked.

'Ah, it is only a mild enchantment to shrivel away your strength, your majesty,' the ogre mocked him. 'You'd better not feel sorry for yourself: I do far nastier things to the women I drag up here. Anyway, there's an easy enough way to break the spell. All you have to do is come back in exactly a year's time and tell me the answer to this very simple riddle: What does every woman long for?

Then he turned his back on the king, stomped inside the fortress and slammed the door.

The Knights of the Round Table were smitten with horror when their king finally managed to stagger back to Carlisle, bent and broken with sickness and despair. He took to his bed and lay there in a shameful torpor, day after day, and then month after month. None of his wise men or healers – not even Wizard Merlin himself – could find a way to cure him.

His illness cast a blight over the whole kingdom. That summer, there was no rain and the crops failed. Robbers and wolves crept out from the Great Forest and brought terror to the land. And by Wadlyn Tarn, the shadow cast by the cruel, misogynous ogre grew ever longer and darker.

If only someone could solve the ogre's riddle! Every day Arthur called his entire court around his sickbed and urged them to try: 'Surely, between you all, you can work out what every woman longs for?'

'Judging by my wife, I reckon it's gold and jewels,' said one knight.

'No, no; mine just wants the most expensive dresses,' sighed another.

'Not material things,' said a third knight. 'In my experience, every woman longs to be flattered.'

'Rubbish!' said a lady. 'What use is empty flattery? What I'd like is a really rich husband – and then for him to die quickly and leave me all his fortune!'

'Speak for yourself,' said a haughty old dame. 'The only thing *I* long for is a bit of respect.'

And so the arguments ran on and on. But not one person in all the court could agree with another.

The year turned: summer faded into autumn, which then hardened into a bitter winter. New Year grew closer, and with it the king's only chance to escape his bewitchment. Finally, he said:

'Good knights, it seems to me that the only solution is to organise a quest to seek the answer to the riddle. So I command you all to ride forth into the Great Forest, each man alone, and let none of you return or rest until at least one man has found it.'

So the knights set out. Some rode eastwards through the winding paths of the forest, some rode westwards, and others went south or north.

At that time, the Great Forest was like no place you will find anywhere in England today. For its ancient trees and creepers spread to the horizon and even further, and it was dotted with mysterious wells, lonely hermitages, lost bowers and secret caves.

As Sir Pellinore rode wonderingly through it, he caught the sound of distant music – a frenzied, eerie tune played on pipe and drum. He followed it to a clearing and glimpsed there a whorl of ethereal dancers who seemed to fade away into a flurry of snow. Then a hunched shape in a scarlet cloak stepped out from the undergrowth and called to him in a creaking voice:

'Greetings, noble sir! Now, why should our paths cross on such an ill-weathered night, eh? Can it be that I am fated to help you?'

It was an old hag – a hideous, hunchbacked, filthy old woman. Her lipless mouth was drawn into a grimace, revealing blackened teeth. Her squinty, sunken eyes were riddled with bloody veins. Her nose was broken and hooked like an eagle's beak. Her jowls sagged and her skin was as warty as a toad's.

'I know what you're after,' she cackled. 'It's the answer to a riddle, isn't it? Well, *I* could tell you it.'

'Then in God's name, you must!' cried Sir Pellinore.

'Judging by your desperation,' said the hag smugly, 'this knowledge must be very valuable. Don't think I shall hand it out unless you give me something of equal worth in return.'

'I swear the king himself will give you a chest full of gold if you can answer the riddle correctly and free him from his enchantment,' said Sir Pellinore eagerly.

'Gold?' scoffed the hideous hag. 'What would I want with gold? It's no use to me.' She rocked with laughter. 'No, no, young man, it's *you* I want. I want to marry you.'

At this, Sir Pellinore turned as white as the snow that fell softly all around him. 'Impossible!' he cried.

'Then be gone, you spineless wretch!' the hag screeched at him.

And before he could say another word, she disappeared into the blizzard.

By and by the snow melted into rain, while thunder rumbled overhead. In another corner of the forest, Sir Kay rode boldly through the storm, driving his horse on and on until he came to a ruined tower. As he drew towards it to take shelter, the same scarlet-cloaked old hag suddenly stepped from the crumbling stones, her mouth twisting into a lascivious grin and yellow tears dripping from her bloodshot eyes.

'Well met, good sir!' she hailed him. 'I suppose you're on the royal quest too, eh? Looking for the answer to a riddle to save the kingdom and King Arthur's life? Well, I could easily solve it and turn you into the hero of the quest – but only if you marry me first!'

Sir Kay stared at her in horror, shuddering at her twisted, warty face and misshapen body. 'God forbid, you ugly old witch,' he answered. 'Get out of my way and let me pass!'

And he spurred his horse to gallop back into the storm.

Far away from the ruined tower, the rain softened into a grey, swirling mist. Sir Gawain slipped off his horse and led the animal slowly through it, holding his hand before him like one who is blind. Soon he stumbled into the dark, spiky mass of a holly bush ablaze with scarlet berries. At once, its branches parted and the hideous hag stepped out before him.

'Good day to you, Grandmother,' said Sir Gawain courteously.

'It's not a good day for me but a tedious one,' the hag croaked back at him. 'I suppose you're like the rest of them, are you? Seeking the answer to a foolish riddle?'

Sir Gawain bowed his head. 'You are right, Grandmother,' he answered. 'And if by chance you are as wise as you are old, perhaps *you* can tell me: What does every woman long for?'

'I know the answer,' the hag replied in a cunning voice, 'but I'm keeping it secret until I find a knight willing to marry me. What do you say to that, eh?'

Sir Gawain gazed at the hideous hag. He took in her warty skin with grime etched into its lines and wrinkles. He breathed in her foul, ditchwater stench. Finally, he looked into her eyes and saw that, hideous as she was, he had no choice.

'I will do what I must to save our kingdom from evil,' he said, even though his heart was heavy with dread. 'Come, good lady: come back to Carlisle with me at once and let us arrange our wedding.'

With a sweeping bow, he offered the hag his hand and lifted her on to his horse.

When Sir Gawain returned to Carlisle with the old hag and her promise to tell the answer to the evil riddle, King Arthur sent messengers out to find the other knights, and by Yuletide all had returned from the Great Forest. Although the king still languished in his sickbed, the rest of the court celebrated that season's feast more hopefully than any had dared to anticipate.

Six days later, another feast was held. This was to celebrate the ending of the old, ill-fated year – and to mark the marriage of Sir Gawain to the hideous hag. The dancing went on for many hours, with Carlisle Castle lit by a thousand lamps under the silvery midwinter moon. While King Arthur lay groaning in bed, Sir Gawain and the hag were married in the little chapel nearby. Then they retired early to their chamber, for Sir Gawain wished to get the ordeal with his hideous bride over with, and quickly.

The little room had been hastily prepared and was in darkness. As Sir Gawain fumbled to light a candle, the hag said to him:

'Why don't you come closer, husband?'

Reluctantly, Sir Gawain took a single small step towards her.

'For pity's sake!' the hag said. 'A big, strong knight like you can't be afraid of me, surely? Go on, kiss me!'

Trembling in the darkness, Sir Gawain placed a kiss on her repulsive, twitching lips. But – wonders! – they were sweeter than dew on a May morning!

'Here,' she whispered, 'I'll light that candle for you.'

So she did – and by its light, Sir Gawain saw that she was transformed. She had shed her ancient, wart-encrusted skin like a snake. Now she had become a beauteous, fair-skinned, golden-haired lady!

'Whatever has happened?' Sir Gawain cried.

'Husband,' said the beauteous lady,' by marrying me, you have saved me from a bewitchment no less terrible than the king's, which was placed on me by my jealous stepmother. I thank you for it from the bottom of my heart. But there is no time to waste. Let us hurry to King Arthur, so I can answer the riddle that imprisons him.'

So they hastened straight away to the king's chamber, where noble Arthur still lay feebly against his pillows. The Knights of the Round Table and all their ladies came crowding in behind them. 'Who is that lady?' they whispered to each other, and all marvelled when they heard she was the very same woman who, less than an hour before, had been the hideous hag.

King Arthur greeted her warmly. Then he said, 'So, my lady, I believe you can tell me the secret I am desperate to know. What is it that every woman longs for?'

And the beauteous lady curtsied and tossed back her golden hair and said, 'Why, my lord, that is easy. Every woman simply wants her own way!'

At once, every lady assembled in the king's chamber began to nod and laugh and clap her hands, for never had they heard truer words spoken.

King Arthur cheered and applauded with them. Then he called to his servants: 'Help me from my bed. Take me to the ogre's castle, and let me free myself from this spell!'

It was a joyful company of knights who helped their weak-limbed king to mount his horse. They all set out in the snow and sunshine of that New Year's Day and made good speed to Hewin Castle. As soon as they arrived, they rapped their swords upon the grim gates. Out stomped the evil ogre, cursing and mocking the king:

'So, you pathetic worm, are you going to try and solve my riddle? Let me warn you: only one answer is correct, and you only have one chance to try it.'

King Arthur's voice rang out into the snowbound stillness: 'What does every woman long for? It is to get her own way!'

Scarcely had these words left his lips, than the ogre roared as if struck by a mortal blow. There was a deafening clap of thunder; and then a bolt of lightning seared the winter sky and split the battlements of Hewin Castle clean in two. The dark walls came tumbling down around the ogre. He fell amongst the rubble as if he too were made only of clay and dust; and when some knights approached to search the ruins, they found no trace of him at all.

As the castle and its evil master crumbled, strength and valour flowed back into Arthur's veins like melting snow rushing into streams with the winter's thaw. Brandishing Excalibur, he led Sir Gawain and all the other knights back to Carlisle.

And there they all lived for many more years, in glory and in peace.

Tom Tit Tot

· *Suffolk* ·

Tom Tit Tot

here was once a foolish woman who had a foolish daughter, and which of them was worse I couldn't tell you. Anyway, one day the woman set to and baked five fine apple pies, and when they were done she put them on the pantry shelf to cool, then popped out to do her shopping. Her daughter was slavering at the mouth because of the delicious smell wafting through the air, and as soon as the mother had left, the girl sneaked into the pantry to steal a taste. It was so good that she couldn't help finishing off the whole pie, and then another and yet another, until soon she'd eaten every single one of them. Just as she was licking the last crumbs off her fingers, her mother came home. When she saw what had happened, she fell into a rage – and who can blame her?

She slapped the daughter hard on both cheeks and when the girl began to bawl, she whacked her backside with a broom handle, just for good measure. Then the woman went stomping out into the street, yelling at the top of her voice:

'Oh lawd, loverducks! What a glutton I've got for a daughter! That's five whole pies the girl's eaten, all in a single day!'

Eventually she calmed down a bit, but when she turned around to go back indoors, guess what she found behind her – a big, black horse with bells and golden ornaments on its bridle, and on its back sat the king!

Of course, the woman was terribly flustered. She smoothed her hair and dropped a curtsey and muttered a humble apology for not seeing his majesty. But the king waved away her apologies and said,

'Good woman, I heard you saying something about your daughter just now, which sounded very interesting, but I couldn't quite catch the words. Would you kindly repeat it?'

Well, there was no way that woman was going to tell the king the disgusting truth abut her daughter's greed. So she thought quickly and answered:

'Yes, I was just saying, your majesty, what a great spinner I have for a daughter. She's spun five whole skeins of flax in a single day.'

'Good heavens above! Five skeins in one day,' marvelled the king. 'I've never heard of such skill and diligence in all my life. She sounds like a girl in a million. Bring her out, woman: let me have a look at her.'

So the woman went to fetch her daughter, who came out giggling and blushing quite prettily. The king looked her up and down for a few moments and then scratched his bristly beard. 'I've been searching for a suitable wife for some time,' he said, 'and it seems to me that this girl of yours would be just perfect for me. She seems innocent, she's a good looker and, best of all, she's clever with her hands.'

The woman's mouth dropped open in astonishment.

'I think I'll marry her,' said the king shortly. 'In fact, there's nothing to be gained by wasting time, so I'll take her with me now and hold the wedding tomorrow, and after that she can live in the royal palace with me and be my queen.'

The woman and her daughter both gasped.

'But there's one condition attached to the deal,' the king went on. 'For eleven months of the year she can laze about and live a life of unadulterated luxury, and I won't ask anything of her. However, she has to spend the twelfth month spinning five skeins of flax every single day, just like you said. And if she can't or won't, I'll have her executed!'

Now, maybe it was the woman's foolishness, or just her optimistic nature, but she didn't worry at all about how her daughter was going to fulfil this condition. All she could think of was how fine it would be to see her child prancing about in fine dresses and priceless jewels, and for herself to be queen mother. The girl got no say in the matter, but as she couldn't see further than her own nose, she was more than happy with the arrangement anyway.

So the girl packed her bags and went to the palace with the king without delay, and the next day he threw a really grand feast for the wedding. The guests were nobles and warriors and emperors from who knows where and the tables spilled over with rich food and wine. Then the girl settled down into her new life, and before long she'd almost forgotten that she had been born a peasant, because she took to the royal lifestyle so easily. And so the months rolled by, and she grew plumper and prettier by the day. Then, all of a sudden, the first eleven months were up.

'Come with me, my dear,' the king said to her the next morning, and he led her up the winding staircase of a tall tower, to a cold, round room that she'd never seen before. In it there was nothing but a single high window, a wooden spinning wheel, a wooden stool and a big rush basket overflowing with raw flax.

'Sit yourself down here,' the king said – and it wasn't said at all unkindly, for he had absolute faith in his wife after he'd heard her mother's boasts. 'Now get on with your spinning, and make sure you've got five skeins finished by the time it gets dark; then you can come down into the hall for a big meal and a bit of dancing.'

The girl sat down and looked up dolefully at the king. 'Supposing I can't get it finished in time?' she asked him.

'Not get it finished in time?' he answered, and his face clouded. 'Ha! I'll have to send the executioner along to you with his axe and tell him to chop off your head!' And with that he went out of the room and locked the door tightly behind him.

Now to tell the truth, not only was the girl incapable of working as fast as the king had been led to believe, but she hardly knew how to spin at all. She was all fingers and thumbs, messes and tangles, and she'd never completed so much as one single skein of yarn in all her life. Knowing the game was up, she burst into tears. Then, all of a sudden, she heard a soft, scuttling noise like some kind of vermin running around the room. She looked up, expecting to see either a mouse or, even worse, a rat. Instead she found herself staring straight at a dark imp! He was no higher than her knee, with a twisted, ancient face and a stringy tail dragging on the floor behind him.

'What's the matter?' asked the imp in a husky voice. 'Why are you crying?' He was an uncanny-looking thing, but he didn't seem set on hurting her. Besides, she was so distressed and lonesome that she thought any kind of company would be better than none. So she wiped her eyes and told him all her troubles, starting with her mother's rage on the day when she'd gobbled up all the pies, up until that very morning when the king, who had treated her so kindly until then, had set her the task and made his grim threat about what would happen if she couldn't fulfil it.

The imp flicked his stringy tail around this way and that, and blinked at her. Then he said, 'There's no need to worry any more, lassie. You just sit back on the stool and have a nap, and don't open your eyes until I say so. By that time, all the spinning will be done.'

The girl was overjoyed at the imp's offer. But she remembered her mother constantly scolding her greed and saying how nothing in life was ever free, so she said to the imp:

'That's very kind of you, mister, thank you very much; but please could you tell me what you'll charge for the job.'

'I might not charge you anything at all,' he answered, 'if you can guess what my name is.'

'Is that really so?' she said, surprised.

'It is,' said the imp, 'and each day that I come in to do your spinning, I'll give you three guesses. That's three each day for the thirty days of this month, making ninety guesses altogether; but if you haven't found the right answer by the month's end, you'll be mine!'

Ninety whole chances was a lot, she thought to herself – surely there couldn't be more names than that in the whole world! So she agreed to the imp's bargain, settled herself comfortably on the stool and closed her eyes as the imp set to work. She was so tired from weeping, and the noise of the spinning wheel was so soothing, that she soon fell fast asleep. She didn't wake until the sun was setting behind the high turret window; and sure enough, the imp had finished all the spinning and there were five neat skeins of fine linen yarn piled up in the basket.

'You've done it all, like you said you would!' she cried.

'Of course I have,' said the imp, 'I'm a gentleman and always true to my word. Now make a guess at my name, and then I'll be off. What do you think it is?'

'Um ...' she said, 'is it John?'

'It's not,' he replied.

'Then is it William?'

'No,' he said.

'Is it Ned?'

'Wrong again!' cried the imp, and he twirled his tail and spun around so fast that he was like a dazzling whirlwind of dark dust; and then he completely vanished.

Never mind, thought the girl to herself, I've still got another eighty-seven chances. To tell the truth, she wasn't at all worried that the imp would snatch her away – she was just so pleased that he'd got the spinning done for her. And then the king came in and swept her into his arms because he was pleased with all the hard work he thought she'd done. The rest of the evening passed in such a haze of joy that she almost forgot her worries.

The next day dawned and exactly the same things happened. The king took her up to the lonely turret and locked her inside with the spinning wheel, the stool and the basket of raw flax. Then the imp appeared out of thin air, told her to go to sleep and did all the spinning for her. When she awoke she had three more tries at guessing his name, but still couldn't get it right. No matter: there were still another twenty-eight days left, and she was sure to find the answer. But the next day ended in the same way, and the one after that too, and so on, until at last there was only one day to go before the end of the month, when the triumphant imp could claim her as his own.

On the evening before that ominous day, on account of all the work he thought she'd done, the king was in an especially good mood with her. He sat her on his knee and fed her choice titbits, and told her all sorts of palace secrets that he'd never shared with her before. Then, all of a sudden he began to laugh, until he was shaking so much that she almost tumbled off.

'Whatever's the matter?' she asked him.

'I was just remembering a funny thing I saw today,' the king replied. 'I was out with all my knights, hunting in the forest, when my horse strayed off the path and I heard a strange cackling noise. I found I'd come to the edge of an old chalk pit, and when I looked into it, there was the weirdest little creature I've ever seen. It was neither man nor beast, but dark and scuttling like a spider, only with two legs instead of eight and a horrible scraggy tail like a piece of dirty string. And it was dancing around and singing at the top of its voice.'

When she heard this, the girl sat up very straight. 'What was it singing about?' she gasped.

The king burst out laughing again, but when he'd recovered himself he said, 'It was all just silly nonsense, my dear. The words went something like this, I think:

> *Nimmy nimmy not,*
> *My name's Tom Tit Tot.'*

The girl bit her tongue and didn't say another word to the king, but you can be sure she was very pleased about what she'd heard. The next morning – her last day of spinning for the year – the king took her into the turret as usual, and soon the imp appeared, sent her to sleep and got on with his work. When she opened her eyes, the usual pile of five linen skeins were in the basket, and the imp was leering at her with a very evil glint in his eye.

'There,' he said, 'that's done for this year. Now I'll have to let you have your three final guesses because I promised to do so, but as soon as you get the last one wrong,' – he gave a lascivious laugh – 'oh yes, you'll be mine! So go on then, what's my name?'

'Er,' she flustered as usual, 'is it Gideon?'

'Wrong!' the creature mocked her.

'Then could it be Emmanuel?'

'No!' he cried. 'Now, lassie, have your very last go.' And he stretched out his mean little hands, all covered in scars and dirt and warts, and snatched at her skirts.

The girl took her time. She swallowed and said the words silently to herself, because she didn't dare risk not getting them right the first time. Then she took a deep breath, pointed her finger at the imp and whispered very slowly:

'Nimmy, nimmy not,
Your name's Tom Tit Tot!'

As the last word left her lips, the imp gave a shriek so piercing that it must have woken every dead person in the graveyard behind the royal palace. Then he vanished into thin air.

And the girl never saw him again.

The Dead Moon

· Lincolnshire ·

The Dead Moon

eep away from the bog.

It's riddled with unspeakable things. It stinks of death.

There are bogles and rotting corpses; dark, nauseous shapes that weave in and out of the mud like worms.

There are fleshless, grasping hands out there, and disembodied mouths that gape open and suck everything into them. There are ghosts and creeping goblins, witches on cat-back, and treacherous, flickering will-o'-the-wisps.

It's an evil place to pass through, especially at night. Many have been lost there. That's why the moon herself came down here once, to try and make things better. She came in disguise, wrapped in a black, hooded cloak so that every inch of her was hidden, slipping down from the sky like a shadow. Through the shifting vapours of the boglands she drifted, gazing this way and that, shuddering at the foul things that surrounded her.

Suddenly, a cry went up: a scream of horror, melting into agony and anguish. Close by the moon was a man: a big, strong, handsome fellow, who was bawling like a baby as the bogles and spooks sank their claws and venomous suckers into him. They tore off his topcoat and shirt, his boots and breeches until he was naked and blue with cold. Cackling and slurping, they began to draw him down into the bottomless, impenetrable dark of the bog.

The moon couldn't bear it. She threw back her hood and let her light shine out. In its beam, the dark things shrivelled and shrank away, and the man found the strength to flail and struggle. He hauled himself from the heaving mud and kicked out at the monsters that had snared him. Thanks to the good moon, he could now see the path clearly, which only moments before had been lost to him. He ran down it with a cry of joy, heading towards dry land and the village.

But there was no escape for the moon: now the evil ones had seen her, they would not let her escape. They came crowding round, fingering her cloak with their bare-boned hands, snorting poison out through their gaping nostrils and covering her with reeking slime. Twisted limbs shot out to trip her. When she was down, they dragged her into a deep hole and pushed a heavy stone on top.

So the moon was lost.

After that, every night was completely dark in the boglands. Even the stars shunned the sky that hung over those parts. It was terrible for the folk who lived there. Their lives dwindled. No one dared go out after nightfall. They sealed their windows tightly and laid salt, straw and buttons on the sills for protection.

As for the bogles and ghosts and witches, they grew even bolder. They came creeping out of the bog, slithering over mud and grass and right into the village. No one even dared to slip out to the privy at night, for the beasties hung around the houses, waiting for a door to open. It was human flesh they craved, and also human souls. Where else could they sate their hunger, since folk didn't travel through the bog any more?

At first, no one could guess why the moon had stopped shining. But then the traveller she had rescued on that fateful night found the courage to look back on what had happened. He recalled how, just as he was about to die, a dazzling light had saved him. He brooded on the memory. Supposing, he thought, the moon herself had sacrificed her life for him? Guilt overwhelmed him.

He set off to see the wise woman who lived in the ruined old mill. She listened carefully to the outpourings of his troubled soul, then took her Bible from the high shelf, glanced quickly into her mirror, and gazed long and deep into her brew pot. Finally, she told him what to do.

The traveller went back to the village and knocked on his neighbours' doors. He assembled a band of nine strong men. When dusk fell, each man put a stone in his mouth, broke a twig from a hazel tree and grasped it in his hand.

The twilight thickened into darkness. The nine men did what none had done for the past three months: they walked out into the night. Shoulder to shoulder they went, but none spoke or even sighed, for the wise woman had warned them to keep absolutely silent.

They stepped on to the bog. The wind screamed at them. They were surrounded by hisses and whispers. In single file now, they pressed on. This is what they were seeking: a candle, a cross and a coffin.

The man who was leading the way halted suddenly. He nudged the man behind him and pointed. The signal passed quickly back along the line. The nine men all stared ...

For a will-o'-the-wisp was flickering before them: that was surely meant as the candle. It lit up a stump of dry, crumbling wood with two gnarled branches jutting from each side: that was the cross. From its base there stretched an expanse of long, cold stone.

That was the moon's coffin.

The nine men gathered around it. In the ghostly light they looked at each other and nodded, then in unison their lips began to move. No sound came from them, for they must not break their silence. But in their minds, in their hearts, they recited the Lord's Prayer.

They recited it forwards, to honour the Cross. They recited it backwards, to drive away the beasties and bogles. Then they leaned forward together, and heaved up the stone.

It came free with a terrible wrenching and creaking sound, spraying them all – near blinding them – with bog water and mud. For an instant, they caught a glimpse of a pale, luminescent face beneath the stone, filled with unearthly beauty. Then light rushed past them, overwhelming them with such exquisite sadness and joy that each man felt the ground beneath him falling away ...

When they came to, there was the moon, back in her rightful place in the sky! The nine bold men who had rescued her were all lying on high ground. Below them, in the moonlight, the bog lay strangely still.

From then on, the folk who lived around the bogs had nothing more to fear. For the gentle moon was ever mindful of how they had rescued her, and vowed to cast her light most strongly over their own bleak lands for ever more.

Jack the Giant-Killer

· Cornwall ·

Jack the Giant-Killer

 long time ago, the south-west of England was overrun by giants. Never mind how big and ugly they were; the worst thing was, they behaved like a load of hooligans, terrorizing people, digging up the land, helping themselves to livestock and kicking boulders around like playthings. It got terribly difficult for decent, normal-sized folk to grow their crops and make a living.

At first, everyone tried to grin and bear it, hoping that eventually the giants would get bored with their malicious games and go away. But they didn't, and as time went by, things got worse and worse.

One of the brutes took over the island of St Michael's Mount, wading through the sea to the mainland to steal cattle whenever he felt like it, not even bothering whether the tide was in or out. He devoured so many of them that soon there were no cows left in the fields at all, and everyone was beginning to starve from a lack of meat and milk. It was so bad that the local lord took himself up to London and literally *begged* the king to send some men along to help. But unfortunately all the king's soldiers were away fighting a war across the sea, and his knights were too busy fighting tournaments. So the lord went back and issued a proclamation, which stated that if any man could destroy the giant, he'd get paid with a fantastic treasure.

None of the local men fancied the challenge because it was so risky. But a young lad called Jack, a farmer's son who was only as tall as your shoulder, with scarcely a wisp of fluff growing on his chin, reckoned he was born to be a hero, so he volunteered to have a try.

Jack might not have been big or strong, but he was certainly bold and cunning. One night he took his spade, his pickaxe and an old cow-horn and rowed out to the Mount. He crept through the darkness to the giant's hall and listened at the door until he heard the brute snoring. Then he dug a deep pit right in front of it, slipped back into the shadows and blew on the cow-horn as hard as he could.

The noise wakened the giant and he came storming out with a terrible roar. In the darkness, he tumbled straight into Jack's pit, and the way he cursed was so terrible, I wouldn't dream of repeating it! Of course, he tried to haul himself out again, but Jack had the pickaxe ready and quickly chopped off his head. That was the end of giant number one.

Not surprisingly, Jack was mighty proud of himself. As soon as morning came, he swaggered up to the castle, and the lord was very happy to reward him with a pile of golden coins. Jack buried these in the forest, then popped home just long enough to tell his family: 'I'm off to slay some more giants!' Whistling, he stepped out jauntily along the road.

But pride always comes before a fall. Little did Jack guess that a neighbouring giant had heard about his valiant deeds on St Michael's Mount and, being the brother of the giant whom Jack had decapitated, he was determined to get revenge. As Jack sauntered along cheerfully, this second giant was waiting to ambush him. The giant pounced on Jack, shoved him into a sack and dragged him back to his castle. Once there, he locked Jack inside and then went outside to sharpen his knife, ready to kill him.

The giant was only gone for a few minutes, but that was long enough for Jack to burst out of the sack, look quickly around and find a piece of rope. He looped this into a noose, shinned up the wall and hid over the doorway. As soon as the giant came back, Jack dropped the noose over his head and strangled him! And that was the end of giant number two.

Jack felt in need of a rest after such excitement, so he took himself off to a quiet beach and had a fine old swim in the sea. As he emerged, the sound of agitated shouting floated from a cave in the cliffs at the far end of the beach. He ran towards it, and soon discovered the cause of the shouters' distress. The cave entrance was littered with human bones and blocked by a large fire on top of which bubbled a huge cauldron of very suspicious-looking meat. In the gloom of the cave behind it, he could just make out a large crowd of men and women, all tightly bound with ropes and chained to the rocks so that they could not move.

'Run for your life, little 'un,' they called, when they spotted Jack, 'unless you want to join us in the giant's cooking pot!'

'I'll do no such thing!' Jack called back. 'Just hold on a bit longer, and I'll have you all rescued in no time.'

Scarcely had the words left his lips than a sandstorm blew up along the beach, and striding through its midst came the giant of the cave. As soon as he saw Jack, he pounced on him, but our young hero still had his pickaxe, so he reached up quickly and sliced off the giant's nose. The brute squealed like a stuck pig and danced about in agony, so it was a very simple matter for Jack to dart under his feet and trip him up, causing the giant to

plunge headfirst into his own boiling cauldron. So that was the end of the third giant. Jack freed the grateful captives from the cave and strode off cockily down the road.

Now Jack's reputation went ahead of him. All the other giants who lived thereabouts had a conference and agreed that they had best offer him a truce. Jack (who wasn't particularly keen on all this killing) readily agreed. He was rewarded by a friendly invitation from a fourth giant, who begged Jack to be his guest for the night.

Jack eagerly accepted his hospitality and had a wonderful evening, with gigantic portions of food and drink. But on his way to bed, he happened to pass the bathroom, where the giant was splashing in the tub and singing at the top of his voice. The words Jack heard made his stomach turn right over:

> *Though you stay with me tonight,*
> *Before you see the morning light*
> *My club shall dash your brains outright!*

So our young hero dashed along to his bedroom and stuffed a bale of straw into his bed, pulling the sheet over it so that it looked like a sleeping man. He spent the rest of the night hiding in a dark corner. And that was just as well, for scarcely had midnight struck than the giant crept in. He was brandishing an evil-looking club, which he smashed into the straw bale with a cruel laugh and a mighty roar.

The giant was astonished when Jack appeared unscathed at the breakfast table in the morning. He couldn't understand how the lad had escaped him, and was full of admiration for Jack's trick.

'I'll show you another trick if you like,' said Jack. 'Hold on though, what's that strange thing outside the window?'

As the giant turned away to look, Jack poured the porridge from his bowl into a bag, held it against his stomach and buttoned up his coat over it.

'I can't see anything,' the giant said. 'Now, hurry up with this new trick.'

'Oh, it's very simple,' said Jack. 'Any fool could do it. I can cut open my stomach without doing myself any harm, and all the food I've just eaten will pour out. I'll show you, then you can have a go.'

He slashed his knife hard across his coat, where the bag of porridge was concealed, and it all spurted out and spattered across the floor. The giant laughed so heartily at the mess that he could hardly catch his breath.

'Go on,' Jack urged him, 'now *you* try it.'

So, without further encouragement, the fourth giant slashed a knife across his own stomach – and that was the end of him.

Jack went on with his travels, and very soon he found himself at yet another giant's castle. This fifth giant was as big and brash as all the others, but he was of a nervous disposition. It happened to be Hallowe'en that night, and when Jack met him, the giant was trembling from head to toe.

'Oh, little m...m...man-thing,' he whimpered, 'c...c...can you protect me from the g...ghosts and spooks tonight? If you do, I'll reward you with some wonderful g...g...gifts.'

Jack wasn't going to say no to that! He coaxed the giant into the innermost room of the castle, locked him inside it and pocketed the key, assuring the brute that even the worst spook in the land wouldn't be able to get his claws into him there. The giant spent the whole night cowering in his hideout. Meanwhile, Jack ignored the spooks that came scratching

on the castle door and screeching at the windows, and seized the chance to steal the giant's treasure, which he buried in the woods next to his hoard of golden coins.

Next morning, the giant emerged, clapping his hands with joy that he'd survived the Hallowe'en horrors, not guessing for one moment that he had been robbed.

'Come and get your reward for protecting me, brave little fellow!' he cried. He led Jack into his hall, where the wall around the high seat was adorned with armour and weapons. From these, he selected a coat that would turn its wearer invisible, a cap that gave its wearer knowledge of everything, a sword so sharp it could even cut through stone, and some shoes that were swifter than the wind.

Jack thanked the fifth giant, feeling relieved in a way that he hadn't had to kill him, and set off on his travels again.

Jack was making his way along a road bounded by an enormous forest, when suddenly he heard screams coming through the trees. Following the sounds, he came upon yet another giant, who had just pounced on a very beautiful young lady and was now dragging her along the rough forest path by her hair. Concealing himself in his Invisibility Cloak, Jack leaped forward and cut off the young lady's hair with his Sword of Sharpness, freeing her in a single blow. Then, carrying her in his arms, he ran in his Shoes of Swiftness all the way to her castle.

Of course, the giant pursued them, so once the lady was safely inside, Jack dashed out again and sawed a deep cut into the drawbridge. As soon as the sixth giant stepped on the bridge, it split in two, sending the brute hurtling into the moat where he drowned.

Jack stayed as a guest of the lady for a whole year and a day, and some people say she would willingly have married him. But by then he was getting restless. So he set off on the road again and soon came to a weird and wonderful farm. It had been taken over by yet another giant, who had turned all the farm workers into animals! The grunts, bleats and whinnies of these unnatural creatures tore at our hero's heart most pitifully, but thanks to the Cap of Knowledge, he knew exactly what to do. Concealed in his Invisibility Cloak, he crept into the farmyard, seized a magic horn from a hook on the wall and blew it three times.

At once the spell was broken, and the animals turned back into women and men. As for the seventh giant, when he saw how his spell had been ruined, he dropped dead with fury!

After that, there weren't really any giants left, and anyway Jack decided he'd had enough of travelling and adventuring. So he made his Shoes of Swiftness take him to London, where he told the king all about his adventures. The king was so impressed that he offered Jack the chance to become a knight. Jack was quite tempted, but on reflection decided that the chivalric life wasn't really for him. So he thanked the king warmly and said he'd rather go home to be a farmer like his father and grandfather before him. The king gave a roar of merry laughter and slapped him heartily on the back, saying that a great hero like Jack must be free to follow whichever kind of life suited him best.

Then the king presented Jack with a huge chest crammed to the brim with jewels and silver dishes. Combined with the lord's reward and the fifth giant's treasure, this made Jack a very rich man indeed. So he went home to Cornwall and married a local lass whom he'd always had his eye on, and they had lots of children together. And from then until the end of his days, Jack always found that his cup was overflowing.

Dragon Castle

· Northumberland ·

Dragon Castle

 t Bamburgh, by the sea, there looms a dark rock. On this rock stands a castle. And in that castle there once lived a mighty king.

This king had a daughter but no sons, and his wife was dead. As the years went by, he grew tired of having only the girl's company by the fireside, and he longed to marry again. So he rode out through his realm, searching high and low for a woman fine enough to be his new queen.

At last he found a highborn lady who was beautiful, quick-witted and skilled at the charms of love. She accepted the king's marriage proposal eagerly – too eagerly, in the eyes of some. Within days, they were celebrating their wedding, and then the queen took her throne beside the king.

The king was ecstatically happy. For when the queen poured out his wine each night, she always laced it with love potion. But the rest of the court found the queen domineering and hardhearted: they all hated her. The one who hated her most was the queen's new stepdaughter, the princess.

The princess had almost grown up by then, and she too was very beautiful. Also, her grace and gentleness were widely admired. The new queen was jealous of her, and because of this she bullied her. She locked away the princess's jewellery, made her dress in cast-offs and sent her away early from the dinner table, so that the poor girl grew pallid and thin.

One day, a special feast was held at the castle. All the guests who came to it had to swear an oath, praising the king and queen. The nobles and their ladies all queued eagerly at the throne. One by one they fell to their knees and declared:

'You are the mightiest king and the fairest lady in all the world. I swear to honour you.'

Then the king rewarded each with an exquisite gift: a fine sword or a golden ring.

At length it was the turn of a handsome youth whom no one had ever seen before. In fact, the youth was a stranger in the kingdom and had only got into the feast by bribing the guards. He walked to the throne with a jaunty step, and his voice rang out loudly and clearly through the great hall as he declared:

'You are the mightiest king in all the world! I swear to honour you.'

Then he rose and turned to walk away without claiming his gift. The king called him back with an angry shout:

'Hey there, young man, wait! Your oath is only half made.'

The youth made no effort to correct his mistake, and brazenly ignored the queen. He walked quickly to a stool in the shadows where the princess was sitting quietly. He bowed deeply to her, then said,

'My lady, they call me the Young Knight of the Wind, and I have travelled countless miles to attend this feast – all because of *you*. For it is true what they say: the queen is not the fairest lady in the world. You are!'

The princess blushed like a wild rose and gazed up at him in amazement. The king too looked astonished. But the queen leaped from her throne with a piercing shriek.

'Guards,' she cried, 'seize that slanderous wretch! Take him down to the beach. As soon as the tide turns to go out, throw him into a small boat with no oars and set him adrift on the sea.'

The guards seized the Young Knight of the Wind and dragged him away.

'The feast is cancelled,' proclaimed the queen. 'All of you: go home and keep your silence. If anyone dares say a word against me – you too shall be banished from this realm.'

The guests stood up and filed quaking out of the hall. The luscious food on the tables was left untouched. The princess began to weep, and the king went to comfort her. But the queen slapped him away with an angry hiss.

'So, you little hussy,' the queen spat at the princess, 'what do you think of your admirer, eh?'

'He seems both brave and noble,' the princess whispered.

'I can tell you for sure that he is neither,' snapped the queen. 'And what do you think of his judgement? Do you *really* think you are the fairest lady in the world?'

'That isn't for me to answer,' the princess replied.

'Indeed!' said the queen crisply. 'So I shall answer it for you – not with words but with deeds.'

Behind the throne stood a table laden with treasures. The queen went to it and rummaged through the treasures until she found a small, black glass bottle and a silver cup. She pulled the stopper from the bottle and poured a dark liquid into the cup. Then she seized the princess, held the cup to her lips and forced the liquid down her throat.

The princess spluttered and gasped.

'Stop!' the king cried, running over to her. He tried to snatch the bottle away, but the queen was too nimble. 'In God's name, are you trying to poison her?'

'No,' said the queen, 'not poison. This is witchcraft.'

'Witchcraft?' exclaimed the king in horror.

The queen gave a demonic laugh. 'Watch her,' she said, 'and you will see.'

The vile brew was already taking effect. The princess writhed about, stretching and squirming in agony. And as she did so, her body began to change. Her dress burst from her. Her smooth white skin blistered, and the blisters turned to scales. Her hair fell out. Horns budded on her head. Claws grew from her hands. She fell on to all fours. Her body grew elongated, sprouting wings and a quivering tail.

The king turned white. At first he could not speak. Then he said hoarsely, 'Oh, you evil witch! How I curse the day that I married you! What have you done to my beloved daughter?'

'You must be even more of a fool than I thought, if you need to ask that,' the queen retorted. 'Can't you see with your own eyes? I've turned her into a dragon!'

Meanwhile, the Young Knight of the Wind had been bound, gagged and cast away on the sea. A fierce storm had blown up as soon as he was set adrift: this too was due to the queen's witchery. At first he feared he would be broken to smithereens on the rocks of the Farne Islands. But he had been born with luck on his side, and he found himself caught in a current that swept him safely past the rocks and out to the open sea. There he drifted for several days, until at last he was washed up on the distant shores of Norway.

Here the queen's spells were too far away to touch him, and he quickly recovered from his ordeal. He offered allegiance to the king of that land, and was rewarded with food, a place to sleep in his hall, weapons, armour and gold.

Months passed. The Young Knight of the Wind grew taller, stronger and even bolder. But although he thrived in his new life, he could not settle, for he still thought constantly of the princess. He asked everywhere for news of her. At last he met a traveller, newly sailed in from Bamburgh, who told him:

'The queen has turned her stepdaughter into a loathsome, flame-breathing dragon. This dragon is causing chaos all over the kingdom. It's eating all the crops and animals and the people are starving. Also, its fiery breath is burning down all the houses.'

'But the king has many brave warriors in his court,' said the Young Knight of the Wind. 'Why don't they kill this dragon?'

'The king won't allow it,' said the traveller, 'for he can't forget that the dragon was once his beloved daughter. But it seems that the queen will soon overrule him for, due to her witchcraft, she now holds the king completely in her power. She has declared that she will allow the dragon to live in the castle for a year and a day. After that, she'll ignore the king's objections and will certainly have it killed.'

When the Young Knight of the Wind heard this, he knew that the time to act had come. He also realized that although he was a skilled and valiant warrior, this was not enough to overcome the queen. So he hurried to the cottage of an old woman who was famed for her wisdom and knowledge of magic. He gave her a purse of the gold he had earned from serving the Norwegian king. Then he begged the old woman to advise him what to do to save the princess.

The old woman took the gold gratefully. She held a candle to the Young Knight of the Wind's face and studied him intently in its light.

'I can see you are honest,' she said at last, 'so I'll give you three pieces of advice.

'First: when you build a new boat to sail home in, make sure you use wood cut from a rowan tree. It's the only kind that's guaranteed to be stronger than witchcraft.

'Second: when the dragon comes at you, roaring with fire and hatred, your first thought will be to kill it to save your own life. Well, don't. Instead, remind yourself of who the dragon really is. Then follow your heart.

'Third: when your deeds are done and the dragon's gone, there'll still be one more thing to do. Go to the queen, seize the sceptre from her hand and throw it into the waves. I promise you won't be sorry.'

The old woman shut her mouth abruptly and showed him to the door. The Young Knight of the Wind thanked her. Then he hurried away, chopped down a sturdy rowan tree and crafted it into a boat. As soon as it was finished, he set sail for Bamburgh.

As he drew nearer, the sea swirled and seethed with the evil spells of the queen. An unnatural wind blew up and lashed the waves, tossing the little boat this way and that. Thunder rumbled and lightning struck the mast. But the rowan wood held fast and true, and the Young Knight of the Wind reached the beach below the castle without coming to any harm.

As he landed, he heard a loud bellowing and the air was filled with the acrid smell of burning. The sand shuddered beneath his feet. The next moment he was dazzled by the brightness of fire. Above him, the castle seemed to shake. Its gate opened and the dragon came slithering out.

It stood on the rocks in a billowing cloud of smoke. Then it spread its wings and soared into the air. Even the bold Young Knight of the Wind could not help cowering under its monstrous shadow. Three times the beast circled him, before it landed in front of him on the beach.

The Young Knight of the Wind had never faced anything so huge, loathsome and ugly; never in any battle had he felt such fear. He was overwhelmed by a desire to kill it. He gripped his sword and crept towards it, aiming the blade at the monster's heart. The dragon opened its vast mouth and belched out flames, watching him with red, bulbous eyes.

But at that moment, the wise woman's words came back to him. The Young Knight of the Wind turned his gaze from the dragon, and in his mind's eye he conjured up a picture of his beloved princess. Oh, how lovely she had been before the queen bewitched her; how gentle and graceful! With trembling hands, he forced himself to put away his sword.

He inched closer. The dragon stood stock still. The Young Knight of the Wind sweated under its fiery breath. He choked at its stench. Still closer he came. He put out his hands. He brushed his fingers against its warty scales and moved even nearer. Thinking of the princess, he put his lips to the dragon's scaly skin ... and three times he kissed it.

On the third kiss, the dragon suddenly juddered away from him. Its fire fizzled out in a rush of cold air. It began to shrivel and shrink. Its skin collapsed as if its bones were crumbling. The sand gave way beneath it and the beast sank into a gaping hole.

Storm clouds rushed across the sky and blanked out the sun, then a wind sent the sand spiralling up into the air, until the Young Knight of the Wind was almost blinded. When it cleared, he saw a pale figure emerging from the hole, luminous in the stormlight. Then he knew for sure that the evil spell had been broken, for it was the princess.

She ran to the Young Knight of the Wind. He caught her in his arms and they embraced. As they did so, a crowd of courtiers, servants, noble ladies and warriors came swarming from the castle and cheering down on to the beach. At the head of the throng strode the king.

He was as overjoyed as the Young Knight of the Wind to see the loathsome dragon gone and the princess back in her true shape. He offered the Young Knight the princess's hand in marriage and half his fortune, too. The Young Knight was eager to accept – and so was the princess! But before they could shake hands on it, the cheering crowd fell silent. For the evil queen had come down to the beach.

The queen raised her hands and began to mutter the words of another venomous spell. But the Young Knight of the Wind knew now that *his* will was stronger than hers. He strode up to her, snatched the sceptre from her hand as the wise woman had advised him, and hurled it into the sea.

At once the queen was devoured from inside by her own witchery. She began to spin round so fast that no eye could follow her. When the spinning finally slowed and then stopped, the queen had gone. In her place crouched an ugly, croaking toad.

And that was the end of the queen: all her powers of witchery were dead. In her toad shape she crawled away to a damp ditch. There she had to lurk, piteous and despised, living on flies and beetles, until she died.

As for the Young Knight of the Wind and the princess, they got married without delay, and very happy they were too. When the princess's father grew too old to reign, the Young Knight of the Wind became the new king, and everyone said that he ruled the land with great generosity and wisdom.

Robin Hood and the Golden Arrow

· Nottinghamshire ·

Robin Hood and the Golden Arrow

 he tables were laden with food and the goblets overflowing with wine, the fire was blazing, and three-score noblemen and women were assembled expectantly in the great hall. At last the sound of hooves was heard, clattering into the courtyard.

Then suddenly the door burst open and in walked a white-bearded knight.

'Sir Richard of the Lee!' exclaimed the lord of the castle, rushing forward to meet him. He greeted the old champion warmly, and then led him to the high table.

The feast began, and a fine one it was too. As soon as it was over and the dishes cleared away, the lord of the castle called for silence. Then he turned to the old knight saying, 'Sir Richard, my guests have travelled here from far and wide, longing to hear your story. Will you begin?'

'My story?' smiled Sir Richard. 'Well, I hope you're not expecting romance or a legendary epic, for I'm no ballad-maker. There's only one tale I know how to tell, and that's a true one.' His eyes twinkled. 'It's about the time, long ago, when I found myself entangled with that infamous outlaw, Robin Hood.'

As soon as he spoke this name, a great noise rippled around the hall. It seemed that half the guests were hissing, and the rest were cheering. Sir Richard held up his hand until they fell silent again. Then he began to tell this extraordinary tale in a loud, unwavering voice ...

Many years ago, when good King Edward still sat upon the throne, my
eldest son got himself into trouble. In entering a tournament, he went
beyond what was permissible and actually slew his adversary; because of
this he found himself liable to pay, as blood money, no less than four
hundred pounds. The boy was barely twenty summers old at the time and
had no way to raise such a vast sum himself, so of course he turned to me.
But all my own funds were tied up, so I was forced to obtain a loan. A
wealthy abbot of the Church lent me the money, with the condition that it
must be paid back within the year.

Unfortunately, one misfortune led to another and by the time the
repayment was due, I had lost many of my other funds and chattels and
found myself almost penniless. So I set off to beg the abbot for further
time, travelling by the lonely forest road in the hope of avoiding all my
former associates, for I could not bear to be seen in my newly impoverished
state. Of course, it was foolhardy to go that way, especially when dusk was
already falling and the wolves were howling, so I was scarcely surprised
when a band of thugs suddenly leaped from the trees and pounced on me.

There was no time to protest, or to prove that I possessed neither the
money nor valuables to justify their ambush. They threw me from my
horse, blindfolded me and manhandled me down a long and winding path
through the trees. When at last I was permitted to see again, I found myself
in a large forest clearing, where the night was lit up by the flames of a
roaring fire. Many men sat around the fire, each similarly dressed in tunic
and breeches, which the firelight revealed as a curiously vivid shade of
green. Only one lady sweetened their company, a beautiful wench with
tumbling hair and rosy cheeks, though I was somewhat outraged to see

that she too was dressed as a man. Beside her sat a tall fellow who, by his very bearing and directness of gaze, was unmistakably their leader.

He rose to his feet and greeted me with a crooked smile.

'Good morrow, friend knight,' said he.

'Robin Hood?' I gasped – for at that time, the whole country was thick with rumours of him, and I had no difficulty in guessing who he was.

He roared with laughter and asked me what I called myself. I told him my name with a quaking heart, wondering what tortuous punishment he would inflict when he realized that I had nothing of worth for him to steal. But I had misjudged him. Robin Hood looked me up and down in the firelight, taking in my ragged clothes and empty purse with a measured eye. Then he shook my hand in a most friendly way and invited me to sit down.

I was allowed to share the outlaws' meal of roasted venison which, they revealed, had been poached from the Sheriff of Nottingham's private estates. The lady served it to me with her own hands; I discovered later that she was Marian, Robin Hood's mistress, though he treated her more like a respected, lawful wife. When we were done, Robin Hood asked what had brought me so low, despite the obvious privilege of my birth, so I told him my sorry story.

'You have my sympathy,' he nodded. 'I admit that in my youth I was even more wayward than your son, and no doubt caused my own father as much grief as your son has brought to you. Let me atone for this by helping you.' Then he turned to one of his followers, a stringy, red-haired fellow, saying, 'Will, fetch me a money bag.'

Will disappeared into the shadows and came back staggering under the weight of an enormous, jingling leather sack. Robin Hood reached into it and, asking me to name the exact amount of my debt, counted four hundred golden sovereigns into a large purse and handed it to me with an elegant flourish.

I was speechless! In those selfish times, never had I imagined that any man could be so unquestioningly generous. No wonder the common folk regarded Robin Hood as their hero!

Robin and Marian were lodged in a little hut of woven branches just outside the camp, but he invited me to lay my bedroll beside the warm embers of the fire. And so I did, but I slept not a wink that night, so astonished was I by this unexpected turn of events. In the morning I bade grateful farewells to Robin Hood and his men, swearing to repay the loan within twelve months to the day. Then I continued my journey to the abbey and handed over the full amount that I owed the abbot - much to his surprise. After which, I hastily returned home to cheer my dear wife with the news of this totally unexpected turn in our fortunes.

And so the year turned. Now that luck was with me, the money that had drained away from my estate in pursuance of my son's delinquency seemed miraculously to return to my coffers; and when the appointed date came, I was more than able to repay Robin Hood.

I set off once more along the forest path and managed to find my own way to the outlaws' secret camp. I entered to find Robin Hood in fine fettle, sitting before the fire and counting an enormous pile of coins. When I called out, he looked up and greeted me in a very welcoming manner. But once again I was in for a great surprise. For when I held out the purse containing the sovereigns that I owed him, he waved it away.

'No, no,' said he, 'no need to pay me back, my friend. The funds I lent you last year have already been returned to me by another - and doubled since I lent it out. How's that for a good investment?'

'But whoever has returned them to you, Robin?' I cried in astonishment. 'No friend of mine has been authorized to act on my behalf.'

Robin's answer was his usual enigmatic laugh, and then he urged me to feast with him again just as I had done twelve months previously.

After that, I returned to my castle, which stands by the edge of the forest near Nottingham, and resumed my normal, tranquil life. I did not expect to see or hear any more of Robin Hood, though I could never forget I was in thrall to him, on account of the generous help he had given me.

One afternoon I was enjoying a quiet chat with my wife in the chamber where she liked to sit working at her tapestry, when suddenly there came a tumultuous knocking at the castle door. I sent a manservant to open it; and within minutes he returned, wild-eyed and white-faced.

'Master,' he cried, 'I know not what to do! For there is a band of men in the courtyard – a rough sort they look, all clad like some private army in matching suits of brightest green – and they are shouting orders at me as if I were their servant, not yours. At their head is a tall man, a very commanding figure with penetrating eyes ... it seems that he is the outlaw, Robin Hood! He says he is on the run from the Sheriff of Nottingham – and he claims it as his right that you will give him sanctuary. He asked me to give you this as a token of his identity.'

And from behind his back my footman produced a most wondrous and precious thing: an arrow, perfectly formed, wrought from yellow gold.

I was alarmed, furious and afraid, for I had no wish to fall out with the Sheriff of Nottingham, who was reputed to be a cruel and callous man. But I was twice-fold in debt to Robin Hood and my conscience would not permit me to refuse him the sanctuary he so urgently needed. So, with a sigh, I went downstairs and welcomed Robin into my castle. Then, as soon as his men had crossed back over the moat and disappeared into the greenwood, I gave orders for the drawbridge to be raised.

It was not a moment too soon! For before the candles had burnt down a single notch, there came a clamour from the far side of the moat. Peering from a turret window, with Robin Hood smiling quietly beside me, I saw a great army assembled across the water, waving the flag of Nottingham.

'Aha,' said Robin, 'so they know where I am. But they also know they will never be able to capture me from here – unless, of course, you choose to betray me, Sir Richard.'

'You know I would never do that,' I answered, averting my eyes from his penetrating gaze. 'But tell me, Robin, why are they after you?'

He roared with laughter at the naivety of my question.

'Surely you know my reputation?' he exclaimed. 'Surely you have heard of all the rich folk my band has ambushed and robbed upon my orders?'

'But you are also generous to the needy, Robin, like a true Christian,' I reminded him.

'That means nothing to the likes of the Sheriff of Nottingham,' he shrugged. 'Why, he would happily roast in Hell for all eternity if only he could have the privilege of killing me. That is why he contrived such a cunning trap for me. Indeed, I guessed it was a trap, Sir Richard, yet the temptation was so great that I could not resist falling for it.'

'What kind of trap?' I asked him.

'Clearly you are a man who is not often about town,' said Robin, 'or you would have heard the criers and seen the bills posted up to announce an archery contest. The prize for the champion was this golden arrow.'

He took the arrow from my footman, who was hovering nervously nearby, and stroked it fondly.

'A beauteous object, don't you think, Sir Richard?' he asked me. 'And what an ample weight of gold! But it was not just the prize that tempted me: it was the matter of reputation. How could I stand back and let any other man claim the title of Champion Archer? I had no choice, Sir Richard: I was *compelled* to enter the contest. Of course, I won it easily, but no sooner had I stepped up to receive my prize, than the sheriff's treachery was revealed. For at the instant I took the golden arrow in my hand, the brute's soldiers rushed forward with swords drawn, and set upon

me. My own men were there in an instant, but we were not so numerous. Although we fought them off and made our escape, as you can see, they followed us in hot pursuit. Thank God your castle stands hard by the town, Sir Richard – and thank God you are able to offer sanctuary.'

I can tell you in truth that I have never passed time more quickly, nor in merrier company, than when Robin Hood was my guest. Despite his restlessness – for he was ever anxious to return to his hideout in the greenwood, where Marian waited faithfully for him – he entertained me with fascinating talk and wondrous stories of his audacious adventures.

But at last his sojourn was set to end. After four days, I was alerted – by the blowing of a hunting horn on the far bank of the moat – to the fact that the Sheriff of Nottingham himself was there, demanding to speak to me. I went outside, but refused to lower the drawbridge, for he had already revealed his treacherous nature to Robin Hood. Instead we called to each other across the water, and when he ordered me to relinquish the outlaw whom, he claimed, I was sheltering illegally, I was ready with a bold reply that Robin had suggested to me.

'Sir,' I challenged him, 'you may be sheriff and executor of the king's laws, but you have no authority to *make* such laws. On whose word do you charge that it is illegal for me to shelter this man, who was so savagely set upon when he innocently stepped forward to claim the prize that was rightfully his? The only laws I obey come from the king. So if you wish me to hand Robin Hood over to you, you must ride to London forthwith, and obtain an order from the king himself to this effect.'

This ploy had the desired effect, especially as my own archers were stationed at every window, ready to fire should the sheriff's men attempt to swim the moat and storm the castle. To my great relief, the pompous villain quickly withdrew, and word came that he had indeed gone to lodge a plea with the king.

As soon as Robin Hood was sure that the coast was clear, he bade farewell and returned to the forest. I was sorry to see him go, for he had lightened my days like no other guest I have known before or since. But I was relieved, too, for I did not relish the danger brought to me by harbouring an outlaw.

However, my relief was misplaced and short-lived. For within a few days, the sheriff was back in Nottingham, boasting that the king had promised to come to the castle within a fortnight 'to deal with Robin Hood once and for all'. When the sheriff discovered that Robin Hood was no longer lodging with me, his fury knew no bounds, for now he stood to be humiliated if the king had a wasted journey. Unbeknown to me, he set spies to watch my every movement. One day, when I carelessly set out alone with only my hawk for company, they ambushed me and took me prisoner.

My friends, at that point I believed my days left in this beautiful yet sorrowful world of ours were truly numbered. I was hauled before the sheriff himself who, without any suggestion of trial or Christian mercy, instantly condemned me to death.

But I had underestimated the courage of my dearest wife, who surely stands in the same league as Robin Hood's fearless woman, Marian. No sooner had she heard that I was all but lost to her, than my wife mounted her horse and rode into the greenwood with only a maid for company; and she did not tarry until she had found the outlaws' hideout. Robin himself was not at home, she told me later, but his men lent her a sympathetic ear and promised that Robin would never let an ally of his die needlessly.

Of course, in my isolation as a prisoner, I knew nothing of this. All too soon the day came when I was bound with thick ropes, blindfolded and led out to the gallows. But just as I was stepping up to them, there came the uproarious sound of shouting voices. Suddenly I found myself pushed and hurled about, first this way, then that. I heard a shriek that made my blood run cold, and then felt a knife carefully cutting me free of my bonds. Hastily, I pulled off my blindfold – to be greeted by the most astonishing and uplifting sight.

Robin Hood stood high up on the sheriff's rostrum, proclaiming my innocence to all who watched. And at his feet lay the sheriff, with an arrow through his heart!

The crowd was cheering and clapping as if the kingdom had just won a war. For the cruel sheriff was hated by the ordinary folk of that city with all their might. Then good Robin lifted his sword high – I can still see it in my mind's eye, glittering gloriously in the autumn sunlight – and sliced off the sheriff's head.

And that's the end of my story. After all was resolved, I returned to my wife and castle to resume the quiet life; and my wayward son, chastened by all that had happened, came home too, reformed himself and settled down to marry. I never saw Robin Hood or any of his men again, but my heart still swells with pride when I recall that once he and I were allies, and that I owe him no debts. For surely men must be equals when each has saved the other's life?

And lest there be any doubt about it, let me show you proof of this story – for I know it is sure to impress you.

At this, Sir Richard paused and turned to the leather bag that he had brought into the hall. He produced from it a long, slim object that gleamed and sparkled in the brilliant lamplight.

'Here it is for all to see,' he concluded. 'For the hero left it with me for safekeeping: Robin Hood's very own, prizewinning golden arrow!'

The Weardale Fairies

· County Durham ·

The Weardale Fairies

here was a wayward young girl who lived in Stanhope, up Weardale, and one day she took it into her head to go off by herself, gathering primroses outside the village along the riverbank. It was a foolish thing to do, for the hills above the river were full of hollows and caves, and everyone thereabouts knew that these were riddled with the hostelries and dancing halls of the fairies.

Even in broad daylight, it wasn't long before the child heard eerie music playing on pipe, fiddle and drum. The tune was so wild and hauntingly exquisite that she found it quite impossible to ignore. It spun into her head and giddied her around it, until she was compelled to hurl down the bunch of flowers she was clutching and hurry towards it. Madly she stumbled through the bracken stumps and brown heather, and came soon to a gigantic boulder jutting from the hillside. Running down its centre was a gaping fissure.

By now the music was almost deafening: no longer could she hear the wind and the curlews crying. It was so frenzied that the girl couldn't keep her feet from tapping; her fingers twitched and her head began to nod uncontrollably.

Young as she was, she knew that she must tear herself away, for fear of being lost to this world forever. Yet the pull of the music was too strong for her. 'Don't look, come away!' she cried to herself. But in spite of her fears, she pressed her face to the crack and peered through it. Beyond it, in a thick darkness lit by a mass of flickering, smoking candles, she glimpsed a sight that few have ever seen: more than eighty miniscule people, perfectly formed and richly dressed, yet each no bigger than a hand-width, dancing around the cavern like a swarm of angry bees.

If the crack had been wider or the girl smaller, she would have squeezed through it for sure, but luckily that was impossible. Somehow, she managed to wrench herself away. Scattering her flowers, she ran back down to the valley and along the riverbank until she reached her home.

'Whatever's wrong?' her mother asked when the girl came lurching indoors, for her hair was all dishevelled and her face as white as a sheet.

'I've seen them,' she whispered, 'the Little People!' Weeping and trembling, she told all that had happened.

'You're safe from them now,' the mother tried to comfort her. But when the father came in from the fields, all her terror came seething back, for he certainly didn't agree.

'They didn't see you spying on them?' he quizzed the girl.

She confessed that she didn't know.

'Then we must assume that they did,' he said gravely. 'And that means ...'
'Oh, my precious daughter, we've as good as lost you!'

'How can that be?' she cried.

'They'll come for you,' the father answered. 'Haven't we told you enough times, you foolish child? The Little People can't bear to be spied on. They'll snatch you away as soon as they can.'

'For pity's sake, ask the wise woman if she can help us!' the mother urged him.

The father nodded gravely and hurried out through the twilight to a lonely cottage at the far end of the village, covered in twisting briars and tendrils of ivy. He knocked at the door and was beckoned inside by a very old woman.

He told her all that had happened. The old woman stared into the flames of her fire. Then she turned to him and said,

'They'll come for her tonight, I reckon. At midnight.'

'But surely there must be some way to save her?' he exclaimed.

'Oh indeed there is,' she said, 'and it's simple enough, yet harder than you might think. For the fairies won't be able to touch her so long as your house is totally silent. However, should they hear even the slightest whisper, they'll snatch her away.'

The father was somewhat comforted. He rushed home and sent the girl to bed at once, strictly forbidding her to call or cry out or make any kind of noise. Then the parents went around the house together. They extinguished the fire to be sure there would be no crackling or shifting, jammed all the clocks so that they could not tick, and overfed the dogs and cats until they all fell into a deep, satiated sleep. Finally they bolted the doors tightly and sat down in the cold kitchen to wait.

After a while, though the clocks were all still, they guessed it must be midnight, for they heard the sound of high-pitched, reedy voices, the clinking of bridle bells and the soft clip-clopping of shrunken hooves. A whole troop of fairies came riding into the yard, but the door was shut firmly against them. The mother and father sat still and quiet as corpses, scarcely daring to breathe.

But however much care one takes, something always slips through. When the girl had gone upstairs to hide in her bed, the youngest dog – hardly more than a pup – had sneaked up with her, missing out on the feast that had sent all the others into slumber. Now he lay at the foot of her bed with one ear cocked. When the fairies opened the gate, he began to growl, and as they pranced across the yard, this turned into a frenetic barking.

The parents looked at each other in horror, and went running up the narrow stairs to the room where they had left their beloved daughter. But it

was too late, for the protective spell had
been broken. The bed was empty.

The child was gone.

The mother wept bitterly all night, but the
father went straight back to consult the
wise woman. She shook her head when she
heard what had happened, but passed no
judgement. Instead, she said:

'It is still not too late to save your
daughter, if you dare to visit the fairies'
cave yourself.'

'Of course!' the father cried. 'Anything!'

'When you go, you must take them three
gifts,' the wise woman went on. 'Firstly,
something that gives light without burning.
Secondly, a piece of an animal's body, which you have taken without shedding
even a drop of blood. Thirdly, a chicken that has no bone in its body.'

'But what does this mean?' the father cried. 'My heart is broken: how
can you expect me to solve these riddles?'

'Look and you will see,' the old woman answered. 'Listen and you will
hear. And wherever you go from now on, carry a rowan sprig with you, for
it has power to protect you from malicious enchantments.'

Then she showed the father to the door and shut it firmly behind him.

A spreading rowan tree stood by the wise woman's garden gate. The
father broke a twig from it and put it in his pocket. Then he set off,
morosely, along the road to his home.

His thoughts were all befuddled and he wasn't looking where he was going, so he didn't see the ragged tramp in his path until they collided. The father offered his apologies and, to make amends, pulled a silver sixpence from his pocket and pressed it into the tramp's grubby hand. The tramp stared at him with sunken eyes, then beckoned him closer.

'My fault, too,' he said. 'If I take this money, I owe you a favour in return. Is there something I can do for you?'

The father shook his head sadly. 'I don't suppose you can solve a riddle for me,' he said. 'Can you tell me what gives light without burning?'

The tramp laughed. 'That's easy for a man of the road like me. The answer is a glow-worm! I often use one to light my way. Here.'

He reached into the hedgerow, scooped up a small beetle that shimmered with a luminescence so soft it could scarcely be seen, and pressed it into the father's hand. 'Whatever you need it for, I hope it works,' he said, 'and may good luck be with you.'

They went their separate ways. As the spring sunshine bore down, the father noticed a movement in the grass. A bronze-coloured lizard was struggling to free itself from a twist of wire. He crouched down to free it. As the lizard scurried away, its tail came off in his hand, leaving neither wound nor blood.

Ah, he thought, putting the tail in his pocket, that's the second riddle solved too.

He continued on his way. In a copse by the roadside, he heard a great squawking. Parting the branches, he saw a thrush besieged by a kestrel. Quickly, he found a pebble and hurled it at the larger bird. As the kestrel flew up and away, the thrush broke into a sweet song, and in the purity of its notes, he seemed to hear these strange words:

Three days by five days
on egg sits hen
chick within
no bones by then.

He hurried home and told his wife all that he had seen and heard. Luckily, one of their hens was already broody, so they set her to sit upon a new-laid egg straight away. When fifteen days had passed, the father took the egg from her nest and added it to the glow-worm and the lizard's tail that were already in his pocket. Then he set off to the fairies' cave.

He trod the path his poor, lost daughter had followed, along the riverbank. Like her, he caught the strains of eerie music, and was drawn to the boulder on the hillside, where a crack marked the entrance to the fairy realms. His anguish was enough to banish his fear. Holding the rowan twig firmly in his hand, he roared out above the deafening music:

'GIVE ME BACK MY DAUGHTER!'

At once the music stopped. In the heavy silence that followed, he put his eye to the fissure and saw the girl. She was dressed in her nightgown, as when he had last seen her, but she was pale as bones now, and held firmly in the grasp of a dozen miniscule hands.

A reedy voice called : 'What will you give us to get her back, mortal?'

'I bring you a light that does not burn, part of a creature's body taken without shedding blood, and a boneless chicken,' the father answered. He crammed the curious gifts through the crack, pushing hard until he heard each one drop to the floor of the cave.

There was a burst of cackling laughter and a flash of light, and then the crazy music started up again. In despair he turned away, thinking that, after all, he would never get his daughter back.

But then ... there she was, standing right behind him, safe, alive and free!

The Devil's Bargain

· *Lancashire* ·

The Devil's Bargain

 Three boys were fooling around in a ruined house, when they came to a door they had never seen before. Pushing it open, they found themselves entering what seemed to be an ancient private library. The roof had not yet fallen in on this little room, and the shelves were still intact and crammed with musty books. The boys pulled some down at random, but were disappointed to find they were all written in Latin.

However, just as they were about to leave the room, their eyes were caught by an exceptionally small volume lying on the floor in the corner. Its black leather cover was embellished with gold leaf and inscribed with the title, *Ye Boke of Moste Ancien Magyke.*

The eldest lad seized it, laid it on a broken table and flipped it open, releasing a cloud of dust that set them all choking and coughing. As this cleared, they saw that, as the title suggested, it was a book of spells.

Most of the charms it contained were of no interest to them, for they concerned such adult and female matters as wooing a sweetheart or easing the pain of childbirth. But on the very last leaf they found a much more interesting heading:

> *A charme to call up ye Devile*
> *Being recommended only to those*
> *Who be foolhardie and willinge to selle their soules to hyme.*

'Let's try it!' cried the youngest boy.

'Don't be daft – it'll kill us!' scoffed the eldest.

'You're just a coward,' retorted the middle one. Then, with the younger boy, he began taunting the eldest one about his timidity and feebleness.

The eldest boy realized that the only way to silence them was to take up the challenge. So he placed the book open on the floor before him and began to follow its instructions. First he moved his left arm through the air in a wide arc, one way and then the other. Then he muttered some weird, incomprehensible incantations. Finally, in a low voice, he recited the Lord's Prayer backwards.

Scarcely had the last word left his lips than there was a creaking noise behind him, and the lad saw the eyes of his two friends widen with horror. He whirled around.

One of the flagstones that covered the floor tilted upwards, until it was levitating several inches off the ground. In the void beneath it was a wisp of pungent yellow smoke. And then suddenly there emerged a dark and sinister head with a sharp goatee beard, and two horns sprouting from its crown.

'So, my young friends, you called me, did you?' it said in a repugnant yet syrupy voice. 'I suppose you think this is some kind of joke, eh? Well, let me warn you, I have no sense of humour. And I am *starving* for human souls. Oh, you may flee me if you wish, but you can never send me away!'

The three lads didn't wait to hear any more. Clutching each other and trembling, they rushed out of the secret room and slammed the door tightly shut. Behind it, they could hear the creature laughing to himself.

'It's the devil!' cried the middle lad. 'Quickly, block it up so he can't get out!'

They set to work, heaping up piles of rubble until the door was no longer visible.

Then they went home, pledging to tell no one of the dangerous sin they had committed, hoping and praying that they would never see or hear of the Devil again.

But the Evil One cannot be dismissed so easily. Having been invited into the village, he was determined to stay. A blocked door was no hindrance to him. He passed easily through it and, as darkness fell, set out to explore.

Every step he took was laden with trouble. He slunk around the houses, rattling windows and doors, and dropping pebbles down chimneys. He prowled the streets, keeping his identity hidden under a vast, black, hooded cloak but sending shivers through every person who met his cold-eyed stare. He skulked through the churchyard, scrabbling up graves with his cloven hooves and knocking down tombstones with his tail.

It wasn't long before the whole village knew that the Devil had come amongst them, and everyone was stricken with terror. A delegation went to the vicar, begging him to exorcize the Evil One; but the vicar, being old and nervous, wrung his hands, saying he had neither the strength nor the courage to take on such a powerful opponent. In despair, they sought help from the only other educated person in the village: the schoolmaster.

The schoolmaster hummed and hawed and tried to make excuses, but in the end they persuaded him that he was the only hope. So he went into the school hall, locked all the doors and windows, and cleared all the furniture out of the way except for his own desk. On this, he placed a Bible. Then, gripping the Bible tightly with both hands, he cried in a tremulous voice:

'May the Devil appear before me!'

At once, there was a loud thunderclap and the room filled with acrid yellow smoke. As it melted away, a grotesque horned creature was revealed to the panic-stricken schoolmaster. The Evil One's cloak was thrown back across his shoulders, clearly displaying his hairy goat-legs, cloven hooves and twitching tail.

'Did you call me, master?' he simpered in a feigned falsetto voice.

'I ... I ...' stuttered the schoolmaster.

'WHAT?' – the Devil's tone sank to a gravelly roar – 'Do you think I am some kind of pantomime genie that you can call up at whim to grant your infantile wishes? Don't you realize the depths of my depravity and the darkness of my power? Aren't you afraid that I shall torment your soul and tear it apart bit by bit, day by day, until the end of time in the fires of Hell?'

'No, no, it isn't like that, sir,' the schoolmaster managed to blurt out. 'It's just that ... I want to ask you ... on behalf of all the villagers ... if you would very kindly go.'

'GO?' bellowed the Devil. 'Kindly? Why should I go if I don't want to? What does a fiend like me know of kindness? Is this a game, by any chance?'

'Of course not sir, it ...'

'But I like games, my friend, especially *gambling* games,' the Devil interrupted. 'Go on, you're tempting me, you naughty boy!' He let out a shriek of high-pitched laughter, then fell to growling again.

'I tell you what, my friend, I'll give you a chance. Set me three challenges: make them as difficult as you can. If I achieve all three, then

83

I've won and you – body and soul – will be mine. But if I fail even one of them, you are the winner – and I swear by every tortured sinner that feeds the infernal flames, I shall leave this village forever.'

The schoolmaster let out a silent sigh of relief. He had expected not only to fail in his mission, but also to fall prey to the Devil almost at once. And, being a physically puny man with unusually sharp wits, he was glad that the challenge did not demand brute strength from him, but cunning. He closed his eyes and ran his hands over the cover of the Bible, desperately trying to think of some impossible task that he could set the Devil to do.

The Devil hovered before him, sucking his teeth with a rhythmic slurp, letting out shrill cackles, clicking his hooves together and fiddling with his tail.

At last the schoolmaster said, 'Here is my first challenge, sir. Go outside and count all the raindrops on the hedgerows of this village.'

Before the last word had even left his lips, the Devil had zipped out through the sealed doors of the schoolroom – and then suddenly there he was again, doubled over with hysterical laughter and chanting: 'Seventy-three billion, four hundred and twenty thousand and eighty-nine!'

Of course, the schoolmaster had no way of knowing whether the answer was right or wrong, so he had to accept it. If only he could think of a task that would take so long to do that all the villagers would be long dead and safely buried before the wretch could complete it! Being a mathematician at heart, he seized on another calculation:

'Go out and measure every stalk of wheat in the big field behind the rectory, then work out to the nearest quarter-inch how many square feet of space it will take up in the barn when it is fully grown, harvested and dried.'

Again, the Devil was off before he could complete the instruction – and back in an instant with an answer that sounded very likely and was impossible to disprove.

'It's no good,' thought the schoolmaster. 'I need to get away from mathematical tasks and think laterally. What other subjects are there? Not History or Latin – there's nothing challenging in those. Ah! Maybe I should be thinking more along the lines of handicrafts. Yes, that's it.'

He cleared his throat and said, 'For your last task, sir, I want you to go down to the beach and weave a rope out of sand.'

Already the Devil was spinning and pulsing as if about to disappear again. But the schoolmaster interrupted him:

'Wait! I haven't finished yet. Then you must bring the sand rope here, wash it carefully under the tap at the sink in the corner and hang it up in one piece to dry.'

The Devil shot him a sly look from his left eye, then, with a flick of his tail, he was away. Almost before the schoolmaster could blink, he was back again, carrying a long, snake-like rope woven entirely out of sand.

'Now wash it!' the schoolmaster commanded him boldly.

The Devil sidled over to the sink. He turned on the tap. He entwined the sand-rope in his claw-like fingers and held it under the flow of water.

At once the packed sand disintegrated into an infinite number of separate grains. The Devil gave a screech as if he had been stabbed through the heart. As the noise died down, the acrid yellow smoke that had heralded his coming began to billow about the school hall again.

And then, in a flash, the Evil One vanished from the village for ever.

The Princess and the Fool

·Kent·

The Princess and the Fool

here was once a King of Canterbury whose only child was a daughter as sharp-witted as she was beautiful. Many young noblemen from far and wide came courting her, so the princess could afford to be choosy. After lengthy consultation with her father, she decided that the only way to select a husband was to test all her suitors with this simple challenge: she would ask each one three questions, and the first man to answer them all to her satisfaction would win her hand in marriage.

So the king issued a decree to this effect, and soon the contest was the talk of all England. Young princes, lords and knights travelled the length of the country to be interrogated by the princess, but the questions (which she always concocted herself) were so masterfully constructed and obscure that none was ever astute enough to answer them.

The king was most disappointed, and resolved to widen the category of eligible suitors to include commoners. Perhaps, he thought, some admirable scholar or rich merchant's son might have enough wit to match his daughter. And so even more young men came travelling to Kent to try their luck.

Amongst them were three brothers who hailed from the wild fells and lakes of Cumbria. Their family belonged to the gentry and two of the brothers were handsome, smartly dressed and well educated; unfortunately, the third had been born a simpleton. His hair was uncombed and his mouth always drooling. To make matters worse, he emphasized his unfortunate condition by dressing in an oversized coat of many colours, and a tall hat shaped like a steeple with a tassel hanging from the top. The simpleton's name was Jack.

Jack's brothers did their best to dissuade him from accompanying them, but fool as he was, his will was strong and he absolutely refused to be excluded. So all three made the arduous journey down the highways and byways of England towards Canterbury, and whilst his elder brothers spent much of the time grousing and grumbling, Jack was always chattering to himself and laughing.

Every so often, the brothers' irritation boiled over and they yelled at Jack to be quiet. Jack always did his best to oblige and, as a distraction, he took to picking things up from the ground and stuffing them into the pockets of his ridiculous coat. By the time they all reached Canterbury and knocked at the palace gates, Jack's pockets were bulging with mysterious lumps.

The palace guards welcomed them in and showed them straight to a room where the princess was sitting, watched over by her father. The two elder brothers fell to their knees and each presented her with a huge bouquet of flowers; foolish Jack just stood there, goggling at her.

The princess turned her dark, long-lashed eyes on him.

'What are *you* staring at?' she asked him coldly. 'And yes, that is my first question, and for goodness sake, don't you dare repeat the old, tired lines about admiring my beauty, or I'll have you thrown out at once.'

'I wasn't going to say anything of the kind!' retorted Jack indignantly, quite forgetting to address her as 'Your Highness'. He reached into the depths of his coat pocket and, to the princess's astonishment, pulled out an egg and held it up. 'I was just looking at your bosom, lady, and thinking that it looks hot enough to roast this on.'

'Roast an egg on my bosom?' cried the princess, stifling a giggle. 'Well, that's the most original idea any of my suitors have come up with! But a wretch like you mustn't touch me. So here's my second question: how would you manage to retrieve the egg discreetly once it was cooked?'

Jack reached into his pocket again and pulled out a twisted hazel wand. 'Aw, that's easy as pie, lady: I'd use this crooked stick.'

'Indeed!' said the princess. Those who looked at her carefully could see she was shaking and quaking, trying to suppress her laughter. But to Jack she said sternly, 'How on earth did a huge stick like that find its way into your pocket?'

Jack wiped the dribble from his mouth with a grubby hand and felt in his pocket again.

'It never had to find its way in there, lady,' he revealed, 'because this stick's been in my pocket ever since the day it was born – from this.'

And he pulled out an old hazel nut to show her, all brown and brittle with age, split open at the top. The princess clapped her hands in delight and burst out laughing.

Jack continued, 'There lady, I've answered all three of your questions. So when do you want to get married?'

'Shut up, for goodness' sake, Jack!' cried his horrified brothers. 'No royal lady could even consider marrying an impudent idiot like you!'

The princess shot them a disdainful look and opened her mouth to speak again; but before she could get a word out, the king roared:

'Not so fast, young man. You've done well indeed with my daughter's questions, but that was only part one of the test.'

'Was it?' the princess interrupted him. 'Well, that's the first *I've* heard of it.'

The king ignored her and went on:

'This is what you have to do for part two. Go home and come back in a month's time. Then, you must sit up with the princess for a whole night without falling asleep even for a moment. If you can do this, she will indeed be yours. However ...'

'There's always a "however", isn't there?' said Jack knowingly. 'All right, King, so what happens if I fall asleep after all?'

'Then off comes your head!' the king snapped at him, and who can blame him for being maddened by the simpleton's impertinence?

So Jack and his two brothers walked all the way back to Cumbria, and Jack was unusually silent. As soon as he arrived home, not wanting to be late for his next appointment with the princess, he turned around and set off again for Canterbury.

This time he travelled alone, for his brothers felt totally humiliated and refused to have any more to do with him. And so, since there was no one to prevent him from entertaining himself in whatever way he wanted to, he had great fun diverting from his journey to climb trees, catapult rabbits and paddle his way through every stream and river that he came to.

In one of these rivers, he saw a school of brightly coloured fish. 'Ah,' he said to himself, 'those are almost as fine as my coat!' So he sat down in the water and scooped some up in his hand. Then he shoved them into his coat pocket alongside all his other curious treasures, not caring at all that he was now dripping wet.

Despite all his dilly-dallying, he got back to the palace at precisely the appointed time, and by the welcome he received, you'd think that the king was pleased to see him. He was taken into the princess's private chamber and seated at a table laden with delicious roast meats, cake and wine. The princess sat down opposite him and picked daintily at her bird-sized helpings. But Jack stuffed himself full and drained the wine flagon down to the very last drop. By the time he had finished, he couldn't stop yawning and his eyes seemed to be closing of their own accord.

'Ahah!' the princess cried, 'I've caught you napping, Jack. That means you've failed the test.'

'Napping?' countered Jack. 'Me? Never! I was just concentrating on my fishing.'

'Don't be ridiculous!' scoffed the princess. 'There's no fish pond in this chamber.'

'You've forgotten my magic pockets,' replied Jack. 'That's where I do *my* fishing.'

And he reached into his pocket and pulled out first one fish, and then another, until he had dropped a whole pile of them into the princess's lap.

'Oh Jack,' she said, 'I've never met such an original man in all my life! Lie down now and go to sleep, and don't you worry about anything, because when my father comes in the morning to see if you have passed the test, I'll make all the excuses needed to save your life.'

So Jack stretched out on the princess's bed and at once fell into an slumber. When he awoke in the morning, the first thing he saw was the glint of the executioner's axe. And the first thing he heard was the king saying,

'Only just this minute dozed off? Stayed up all night catching fish from his pocket? I've never heard such nonsense! Get out of the way, daughter, and let the executioner be done with this idiot.'

'Now hold on, King,' Jack spoke up at once. 'Have you never heard of pocket-fishing? It's the latest fashion, you know, a very fine sport that I learned from none other than the King of France. Just step over here, sir, if you don't mind, and I'll teach you how to do it.'

So the king got out of his chair and reluctantly went over to Jack, and while the king was harrumphing and complaining and looking the other way, Jack put his hand back into his coat pocket and secreted a fish in his fist. Then he made great show of pushing this fist into the king's pocket, pricking him through the fabric with his fingernail as he did so, and pulled the fish out for all to see.

'Sorry if it nipped you when it was biting its bait, King,' he said.

The king, after he'd got over his outrage and astonishment, found himself spluttering and guffawing. Before he could stop himself, he began laughing every bit as loudly as the princess herself.

By the time they had both managed to calm down, they found that the Lord High Chancellor had sneaked in to see what all the noise was about, and Jack had taken him aside and was already discussing plans for his wedding. Indeed, it took place the very next day, and never had England seen such an extraordinarily dressed bridegroom as Jack in his multicoloured coat and tall, tasselled hat.

I'm very happy to tell you that Jack and the princess enjoyed a fine old marriage in which every day was filled with laughter. When the king lay on his deathbed, he could think of no one better than his eccentric son-in-law to name as heir to his kingdom.

The Seventh Swan

Swan

· *Cambridgeshire* ·

The Seventh Swan

he swans came down suddenly with the winter dusk –
huge and white, all seven of them, dropping from the
heavy sky as if crystallized from snow. The fen was
awash; icy mud and water mingled amongst the dead
reeds. To the west, the sky was bloody with the last
streaks of sunset. To the east lay only more wetland and the dark.

The people who lived around the fen were hungry. All year there had
been too much rain, so the crops had failed and there was no fodder for
their pigs or cattle. A swan would yield plenty of meat to feed a family,
but nobody dared to shoot one.

Swans were forbidden. Nobody knew why. There were rumours of
sinister ancient magic. People were suspicious and didn't hesitate to
believe them.

Except for one: a silent young man, gangling and covered in scars,
with a sour tongue and mocking eyes. We'll call him the fowler. He lived
in a tumbledown hut on the edge of the village: one room with a door
that opened straight on to the marshland. He liked shooting waterfowl.
He was always alone.

The morning after the swans landed, the fowler stepped out and saw
them. Regally they drifted past him, watching him with vacant, yellow-
rimmed eyes. The fowler fetched his gun from his tumbledown hut and
went to lie hidden in the cold, damp reed beds. He took aim and shot one
of the swans.

The victim gave an unearthly screech and keeled over to its side. One wing loomed up over the reed stumps – it was brilliantly, impossibly white. The fowler rose in triumph and began to run towards it, splashing through the muddy shallows.

But before he could reach it, the other swans came at him: six huge, hissing birds, a mass of beating wings and sharp, prodding beaks. The fowler had left his gun in the reed beds, but no matter: he had something even better and stronger. He pulled a hunting knife of heavy iron from his belt and brandished it.

At once the swans withdrew, for like all unearthly creatures, they could not abide the sight of iron. They waddled backwards, then soared from the ground into the air, gracefully flying towards the pale December sun rising slowly in the sky. Only the seventh swan, the shot one, was left behind.

The fowler went to it. It was still early and no one else was about. He thought he would pluck the bird's feathers straight away, then take it home for his cooking pot, before any neighbours found out what he had done and either scolded his foolhardiness or begged for a share of it.

But when he reached the swan, he found that it was still alive. Its wing was badly hurt, but it breathed and squirmed and hissed at him. He fetched a rope from his hut, caught the bird in a noose and dragged it home behind him. When he reached his door, he hesitated at first, then hauled the swan into his single room and let it lie by the warmth of his stove. All the way there it had struggled; now it lay still.

The fowler didn't know what to do. He desperately wanted to kill it and eat it, but now it was in his hut, he didn't have the heart. Instead he found himself fetching clean water, rags and bandages. He bathed the swan's wounded wing and bound it close to its body.

While he went outside to dispose of the soiled water and rags, something extraordinary happened. He came back inside to find that the wounded

swan was gone. In its place stood a girl, maybe sixteen winters old. Her skin was so pale it was almost translucent, her hair the flaxen blonde that one sometimes sees in the lands of the far north. Her eyes were watery and expressionless. She wore a long, plain dress, white and flowing, and her left arm hung awkwardly, with a bandage binding it to her side.

The fowler stared at her. She said nothing. She looked helpless and vulnerable, and in his twisted way he had an urge to treat her roughly. He grabbed her good hand and tried to force her to serve him as if he were her master, but she spat and hissed at him, kicking out and even biting. In the end, he left her alone, and she crouched on the floor all night in the warmest spot in front of the fire.

The next day he went out shooting other wild birds and doing odd jobs. He locked the hut and left the girl there. When he came back, everything was dirty and messy, just as he had left it, and the fire had gone out.

That night he tried to bend her to his will again and failed. When the wind came hurtling across the fens in the darkness, there was a wild knocking at the door. He opened it to see six swans rising from the path, startlingly white against the night sky. He slammed the door against them, and turned back to find the girl shaking with uncanny laughter.

Six days and six nights passed in the same way. On the seventh day, he returned home to find that the girl's wounded arm had miraculously healed. She stood waiting for him in the centre of the ramshackle room. Her body was covered from head to toe in soft, white down.

He took a step towards her, but she put up a hand to stop him. And as he stared, he fancied that the down that covered her was growing. Indeed, soon it had become a luxuriant coat of feathers. Her long hair fell from her head to the floor. Her face elongated and her mouth became a beak. Her neck grew and arched into an elegant curve. Her body contorted, her legs shrank and webs appeared between her toes. Her arms were no more, becoming wings.

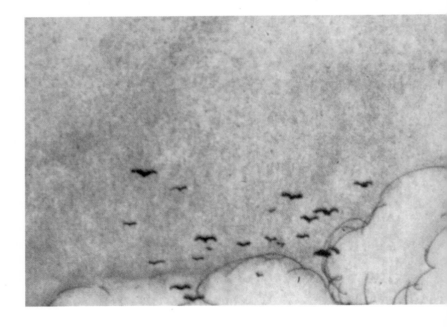

Then the swan-girl flew at him with a terrible hiss. Her wing flapped against him, sharp as sailcloth in a strong gale. Her beak poked and pecked at him. Now she seemed enormous: he cowered under her power, then pulled open the door and fled into the night.

The swan-girl came after him. And six other swans rose from the shadows of the fen and flew to help her. The fowler ran blindly away from them. Soon he had lost the path and found himself wading into the dank marsh water. Now the swans were before him, behind him, above him and every way he turned. Only the water offered sanctuary. Deeper and deeper he waded into it, flinching from the beating wings, deafened by the endless hissing.

Dawn was breaking when the seven swans finally rose from the fen. A hen-wife, coming early from her cottage, swore that she saw them circle the marshes seven times, then fly away into the sunrise.

Later that day, the fowler's body was found, bruised and badly lacerated, floating face down in the pool where he had drowned.

The seven swans were never seen again.

The Knight of York

· Yorkshire ·

The Knight of York

here was a poor cobbler in York who had so many children that he didn't know how to feed them. When his wife gave birth to a seventh child, their joy at the gift of a beautiful girl was overshadowed by despair. 'I'll not be able to wean her,' said that good woman, 'unless I take food from the mouths of the others.' She wept bitterly at this prospect, but neither she nor her husband could think of a solution.

One morning, the woman was sitting in the back of their shop with the baby at her breast when the bell jangled, the door opened and in strode a very grand man dressed in full armour and flaunting a huge sword on his belt. The shopkeeper bowed to him, for he recognized his customer as a famous knight whose wealth and power were the talk of the city. The knight greeted him in a jovial way and, seeing the newborn baby, offered his congratulations.

'Thank you sir,' the cobbler replied gloomily, 'but the truth is, the child's set to bring us more misery than joy. For business is so bad, I don't know how we'll ever feed her. Her brothers and sisters are always hungry.'

'Tut tut,' said the knight, as he handed the cobbler a pair of expensive leather riding boots for repair. 'But maybe things will work out better than you think. You never know, this little girl may have great things ahead of her. I tell you what, I'll look her up in my *Book of Fate*.'

And before the cobbler and his wife could protest (for they were alarmed at the idea of what sounded like wizardry), the knight stepped outside, went to his horse, took a large and very ancient volume from the saddlebag, brought it in and opened it on the shop counter.

The impoverished couple waited nervously as the knight thumbed through the yellowing pages, searching until he found the symbols that coincided with the baby's date and time of birth, and her name. They were puzzled to see the knight blanch as he read through the predictions and prescriptions, and when at last he spoke again, there was a strange tremor in his voice.

'Good people,' he declared, 'your new daughter must not remain a moment longer amongst the shadows and filth of this city. For I read here that she is destined to grow up as a fine lady and hold court in a great country estate.'

The couple's mouths dropped open in astonishment. But before they could utter a word, the knight went on:

'Let me adopt her! Let me take her to my own estate and castle, where she can feast upon delicacies and dress in silk and jewels. Good people, you cannot say no, for how else will she achieve the things that God Himself has planned for her?'

And with that, he snatched the baby from her mother's arms, swept out of the shop and carried her away on his horse.

Now, you might think that this was a wonderful solution for both the baby and her parents, but you have yet to hear of the darkness that warped the knight's soul. For the words he had spoken were lies. In consulting the *Book of Fate* he had really discovered the extraordinary fact that the girl was one day destined to marry his own son, and in his arrogance and conceit, he could not abide the prospect of having a pauper for a daughter-in-law. So he had no intention of adopting the baby, despite his generous promise. Instead, he took her straight to a lonely part of the River Ouse. There he stood on the bank and threw her into the water with a stone tied to her ankle, like an unwanted kitten, to drown.

The guilty knight hastened away from the scene of his crime, and that was just as well. For I am happy to tell you that the baby did not drown after all, but was carried away in the swift-flowing water like a fallen leaf. By and by, the currents brought her close to the bank, where she was spotted by a kindly farmer. He waded into the river to rescue her and took her home to his wife; and this couple took it upon themselves to foster her with great happiness, for they had no children of their own.

So the girl grew up, well fed and contented, and there was not a prettier girl to be found in any of the ridings of Yorkshire.

But no sooner had she passed her sixteenth birthday than someone came knocking at the farmhouse door. The farmer and his wife were both out, so the girl opened it herself. And who should be standing on the doorstep, clad in finery? None other than the Knight of York himself!

Of course, the girl knew nothing about him, and at first the knight had no idea who she was. But in buying a basket of newly laid eggs from her, he became enchanted by her great beauty, and in order to dally with her a little longer, he offered to tell her fortune. The naive girl readily agreed. So the knight drew his *Book of Fate* from his saddlebag, and quickly realized that she was the very same girl he had tried to drown all those years ago – the pauper girl who was destined to marry his son!

The malevolent knight thought quickly. As before, he was desperate to kill her, but now that she had grown into a lovely young woman, he was too cowardly to do the deed himself. So instead he asked the girl to carry a letter to Scarborough Castle, offering to pay her well. The girl liked the idea of earning some money, and accepted the task willingly.

The letter was addressed to the knight's brother. This is what it said:

The girl who delivers this to you will bring shame and misfortune upon my son and all our family. Therefore I urge you to kill her as soon as you have read this, and to bury her body where none may find it.

The girl set out eagerly, carrying the sealed letter under her cloak. Of course, she had no idea what it said. She walked some of the way down the long road to Scarborough, and hitched cart rides too, but by sunset she was still far from her destination, so she sought lodgings for the night at an inn.

The food at the inn was tasty and its beds were amply filled with feathers, but the landlady was forgetful, and that night she failed to bolt the door. So when everyone was sleeping, a thief managed to break in. He crept from room to room, stealing jewels here and money there, but when he broke into the girl's chamber, he found nothing but the letter she was carrying.

The nosy thief couldn't resist opening and reading the letter, and he was shocked. He looked at the lovely girl who lay in all innocence upon the bed, and then back at the letter. His heart – which thought nothing of common or garden dishonesty – was sorely troubled. Theft is one thing, he thought to himself, but murder is quite another! So he took the letter outside and tore it up, scattering the pieces to the wind. Then, finding paper and a quill pen in the darkness of the landlady's parlour, he quickly replaced the letter with another, and this is what it said:

The girl who delivers this to you is destined to bring great honour and good fortune to our family. Therefore I urge you to introduce her to my son as soon as you have read this, and to arrange at once for their wedding.

The next morning, the girl woke up cheerfully. Although the inn was in uproar as the other guests discovered they had been robbed, she had no idea the thief had even entered her room. Clutching the letter diligently, she continued her journey. By sunset that day, she found herself breathing in the salty sea air and knocking at the door of Scarborough Castle.

A servant ushered her inside when he saw she had a letter for his master, the Knight of Scarborough. The knight read it at once, and was less surprised by its contents than you might think. For it so happened that his nephew, the Knight of York's son, was staying with him for a few days, so he was in an ideal position to arrange a liaison. He invited the girl to his household for dinner, and though she had never been in such a grand place before, she conducted herself with perfect manners. The Knight of York's son was entranced by her. The next morning he proposed to her, and the girl accepted. The Knight of Scarborough, mindful of the instructions in the letter, held their wedding before the week was even out.

Of course, the Knight of York hastened to Scarborough to celebrate his son's marriage, but when he discovered the identity of the bride, he was beside himself with rage. To think that all his plans had been thwarted and his son was now married to the pauper girl he despised! He seized the girl, drew his sword and held it to her throat. But for all his show, he lacked the courage to deal the fatal blow. Instead, he threw her contemptuously to the floor. Then, he dragged her out to the cliffs. He pulled the golden wedding ring from her finger and hurled it out to sea.

'There: it is gone,' he cried, 'so you have nothing to prove that you are my son's wife. I forbid you ever to come near my family again!'

'Oh please, sir,' the girl implored him, 'at least give me a chance to see my husband again, for I love him truly.'

The Knight of York gave a snort of malicious laughter. 'Well,' he mocked her, 'if you can retrieve that ring from the ocean bed, I *might* consider it.'

'That's impossible,' the girl wept. 'The sea is too big.'

But the knight turned his back on her and strode off to his brother's castle. The poor girl was left alone, and at first she didn't know what to do. She went into the town and spent several wretched days weeping, begging and sleeping rough. But by and by she pulled herself together and began knocking on doors to seek employment. Before long she found herself a position in a grand house, working as a gentleman's kitchen maid.

One day the gentleman decided to throw a banquet and invited dignitaries from all over Yorkshire. He sent his cook down to the harbour to buy a large quantity of fish, and when she came back she was too exhausted from carrying it to do the cooking. So she told the girl to do it instead. The girl set to with a willing hand – and was rewarded with a truly astonishing surprise. For in the process of gutting a particularly large haddock, her eye was caught by something gleaming. And there in the haddock's stomach, she found her own lost wedding ring!

Trembling with excitement, she washed it and slipped it back on her finger. Then she finished cooking the dinner. Soon the guests could be heard arriving, and amidst the babble upstairs she caught the sound of two very familiar voices. One belonged to her beloved husband – and the other to his father, the evil Knight of York.

When it was time for the fish course to be served, the girl persuaded the serving maid to let her carry in the dish herself. She placed it carefully on the centre of the banqueting table and looked around. She saw the Knight of York at once. She went to him and held out her hand, pointing silently to the ring he had so heartlessly snatched from her, which was sparkling once more upon her finger.

The Knight of York turned white with shock, then purple with rage. He drew his sword and would have slain the girl he despised so much there and then. But his son, who was seated beside him, drew his own sword.

'I will kill you, my father, unless you cease this evil at once and stop persecuting my dearest wife!' he cried.

These words brought the Knight of York to his senses at last. He was overcome by shame. He sheathed his sword and, in front of all the guests at the banquet, begged his son and daughter-in-law for forgiveness.

The young couple were so overjoyed to be together again that they readily agreed to grant it. So in the end, the girl's destiny to rise from poverty and become a great lady was fulfilled, just as had been written in the *Book of Fate*. And despite all that had gone before, everyone in this curious tale lived happily ever after.

The Wicked Witch

· London ·

The Wicked Witch

here was once a devious old witch – and you know what *her* sort are like: always setting charms and jinxing things, and laying cunning traps to ensnare innocent children. Everywhere she prowled, there was a toad on her trail and a curse on her tongue, and you can be sure that nobody wanted to go near her.

Now, in another part of the country there lived an impoverished family with a strapping daughter, and as soon as the girl was old enough, they sent her out into the world to seek employment. She wandered here and she wandered there, knocking at the door of every big house she came to, asking them to take her into service, but nobody wanted her. So she was forced to search even further afield, and before she knew it, her journey had taken her far from home and into the wicked witch's land.

Soon the girl began to notice some very strange goings on. Many of the animals she passed were making noises that sounded like human speech, which she found very unnerving. Then the trees started talking too, and even the rocks; until finally, a disembodied voice screeched out:

'Help me child, oh help me do!'

'Whoever is that?' the girl called fearfully.

'I'm over here, in the field to your right,' the voice shouted.

Turning, the girl saw that an iron oven had been dumped in the middle of the field, and wafting out of it was the smell of burning. She approached it cautiously, and from inside the oven the voice called to her again:

'Pity me, child, for once I was a fine and wholesome loaf of bread. But the wicked witch shut me in this oven seven long years ago, and though I am baked through and through she will not let me out.'

The girl had a kind heart, so she ran to open the oven door and set the loaf free, laying it gently upon the grass. The blackened loaf was gasping for air, but it thanked her profusely and swore that, should the girl ever find herself in similar need, it would do all it could to reciprocate her kindness.

The girl went on her way, and very soon she came to another field where a cow with dangerously swollen udders stood bellowing piteously. As she approached it, the beast ceased its bellowing and called to her in human language:

'Help me child, oh help me do! Once I had two calves to drink from me, and a jolly farmer to milk me when the calves were satisfied. But seven years ago, the wicked witch drove them all away and cast a spell that made me swell and engorge unbearably. I am desperate for relief!'

At once the girl ran to the cow and set to work on her udders until a flood of milk flowed free. The cow vowed that she would never forget such kindness and expressed the hope that she would one day be able to return it.

And so the girl set off again, wondering at these strange events. Soon, her thoughts were broken into by a curious, creaking voice, which groaned:

'Ah me, how I suffer! Help me child, oh help me do, if you have even a grain of sympathy in your heart.'

The girl looked over a dry-stone wall to see a solitary, gnarled old apple tree, whose branches were laden with enormous, misshapen fruits. Some had grown as large as pumpkins, whilst others were rotten and crawling with maggots and wasps.

'Once I was the finest tree in this orchard,' the apple tree sighed. 'But seven years ago, the wicked witch killed all my companions and enchanted me so that I endlessly bear hideously deformed fruit that no one will pick. If only you could free me from this burden!'

By now, the girl was well used to such curious appeals. At once she hitched up her skirt and climbed over the wall. Picking up a nearby stick, she reached up and beat it against the wretched tree's branches until all the malformed apples had tumbled to the ground.

The grateful tree straightened itself and rustled in the breeze, swearing eternal friendship to the girl and earnestly hoping that it would have an opportunity to be equally good to her in return.

And so the girl continued on her way, and the next place she arrived at was the house of the wicked witch. She took her courage into her hands and knocked boldly upon the front door. When the witch herself answered it, the girl dropped her best curtsey and asked the repulsive old hag if she had any need of a servant.

'Indeed I do, yes I do,' the witch cackled, peering down her warty nose at the girl and beckoning her inside with a crooked finger. 'And I will pay you well, child, very well, so long as you keep my little house here tidy and clean.'

'Oh, I will ma'am,' the girl assured her, for she was so relieved that she had at last found a way to earn an honest wage, that she scarcely cared who her new employer was.

'Not so hasty!' the witch snapped back at her. 'I haven't finished talking to you yet. Before you start work, I must tell you the rule of this establishment: you must never, ever look up the chimney – for if you do, you'll regret it!'

The girl promised faithfully to do as she'd been told, and the witch set her to work without further ado. At first everything went very well. But you know how it is when something is forbidden: it makes you long to do it, and it nags and nags at your mind until you can think of nothing else. That's exactly how it was for the girl, who had a burning desire to look up the chimney. Of course, she couldn't do anything about it while the witch was spying on her with those sunken, all-seeing eyes of hers. But one day the old hag went out to attend to some secret business of her own, and as soon as she had gone, the girl took her chance.

She went and stood in the chimney breast and poked her head inside to see what was there. And you'll never guess what she found. Not a spook or a booby trap, but a huge sack of gold coins, easily within her reach! Of course, the girl couldn't resist reaching up and pulling it down.

But at that very moment, she heard the front door creaking open and the witch's outsized feet stomping into the house!

'I'd better get out of here,' the girl thought to herself, panicking, so she opened the window, jumped out and ran for her life, taking the sack with her.

She hadn't got very far when she heard the witch coming after her. But just then she came to the ancient apple tree that she had helped on her outward journey. As soon as the tree saw that the girl was fleeing the witch, it rustled its leaves and called to her: 'Quickly, child! Climb into my branches and hide.'

So the girl did, and not a moment too soon, for the witch was almost upon her.

'Now then, you scabby old tree,' the wicked witch hissed, 'have you seen a slip of a girl running off with my treasure?'

The tree swayed and creaked and groaned, saying: 'No, mother, not for seven years.'

So the witch went on her way ... hah, but it was the wrong way! Meanwhile, the girl climbed down from the tree, bade it a fond farewell and ran in the direction of her home. And it wasn't long before she met the cow she had helped before.

The cow lowed a soft greeting and licked her affectionately, but then the gentle beast saw that the wicked witch had turned around and was fast approaching in the distance.

'Quickly, child!' she bellowed, 'hide in that long grass where no one may see you.'

So the girl did, and not a moment too soon, for the witch was almost upon her.

'Now then, you fat old cow,' the witch hissed, 'have you seen a slip of a girl who's stolen all my treasure?'

The cow blinked and shook its head slowly, saying, 'No mother, not for seven years.'

So the witch went on her way, and once again it was the wrong way. The girl came out of the grass, bade the cow a fond farewell and ran yet further towards her home. And it wasn't long before she met the loaf of bread she had helped on her outward journey.

The loaf greeted her cheerfully and broke off some tasty crumbs from its belly, offering them to the girl to nibble, but then it spotted the wicked witch, who had changed direction again and was galloping towards them in the distance.

'Oh loaf, whatever shall I do?' the poor girl cried. 'Please can I hide in your oven?'

'No,' the loaf replied, this time you must not hide – but run as fast as you can!'

So the girl ran off, and by the time the witch had reached the loaf of bread, she was three whole fields away and near the horizon.

'Now then, you burnt and crumbly loaf,' the witch shrieked, 'I know you're hiding that thief of a girl in your oven! Move out of the way so I can open the door, pull her out and tear her to pieces!'

'Of course, mother,' the loaf said politely, and it stepped aside so the witch could open the oven door and peer inside.

'I don't see her,' she hissed. 'Where is she, where is she?'

'She must be cowering at the back, mother,' the loaf answered. 'If you go right in, you are sure to find her.'

So the wicked old witch hauled herself up with her claw-like hands, sat in the oven's doorway and swung her crackly, bony knees up, then climbed right inside.

At once, the loaf slammed the door shut. Then it lit the oven so that the witch was burned to a cinder!

As for the girl, she ran all the way home with the witch's treasure. By all accounts, her family was very glad to have her back safe and sound.

The Asrai

· Shropshire ·

The Asrai

id you ever hear about the fellow who was walking to work past a lake in the twilight of a winter's morning, when he saw a woman waving at him from the water? He did a double take and sneaked nearer, and that's when he realized she had green hair, not a stitch of clothing, and was swimming about with a fishtail instead of legs. And no, he hadn't been drinking!

He was torn between getting closer so he could have a really good look at her, and leaving quickly in case she worked some horrible spell on him, but before he could make up his mind, she called out to him, and any intention he had of avoiding her immediately melted away.

'Come here, my love,' she cooed at him, and her voice was as sweet and gentle as the waves lapping through the reeds on the water's edge. He went weak at the knees and found himself running down the bank as if she were pulling him on a string.

'Come right into the lake, my darling,' she urged him, and he stepped off the bank obediently and went wading out to her. It sloped so steeply underfoot that the water was soon right up to his waist, and then his chin.

'I'll give you treasure, my love,' she sang to him. 'Silver and gold and jewels! But you'll have to come closer, so I can put it into your hands.'

Then she dived beneath the surface and reappeared right in the centre of the lake, in the part that some folk say is bottomless. With one hand she was beckoning, and in the other she held up a huge lump of sparkling gold.

The poor fellow could hardly believe his eyes! He swore roundly and loudly at the wonder of it – and that was a big mistake. Because no sooner had the foul words left his lips than the woman dived back into the lake with the gold, and there was no sign of where she had gone.

So he had to go home and change his sopping clothes, arriving late for work with nothing to show for it except a strange tale. Most of his workmates just scoffed at what he said, of course, but there was one old gaffer (who must have been long past the official retirement age) who looked at him very seriously and said,

'You weren't seeing things, you know. That was an asrai.'

'A *what?*' said the fellow.

'That's the proper name for a water fairy,' the gaffer told him. 'Rare creatures, they are – I've never met anyone else who's seen one. They live on the lake bottom where it's cold and dark, but once in a century they come up to the surface to bathe in the moonlight, because that's what makes them grow. Was it still half-dark when you saw her? Ah well, that'll be why she was still out. And it's not surprising your oaths scared her off. They're tricksy things, and they can't stand human coarseness.'

The fellow brooded on these words and his strange experience. He couldn't get the asrai out of his mind. He badly wanted to see her again. So that

night he borrowed a boat and a fishing net, and rowed out on the lake, dragging the net behind him.

After a while, the lines grew taut and when he tested the net, he found it was very heavy, so he hauled it in. Just as he had hoped, there was the asrai inside it!

She was a truly lovely thing, he told everyone later: no bigger than a young lass, but fully formed as a woman above her fishtail, and not showing any sign of wear and tear, even if she was indeed hundreds of years old. Her long, green hair was like trembling drifts of water weed. All his anger disappeared at the sight of her and when she started to cry, his heart went out to her. She couldn't speak clearly, now that she was out of the water, but he guessed that she was begging him to set her free.

And he nearly did. But then he remembered how she'd tempted and tricked him earlier that day, and given him a nasty soaking, so he steeled himself and resolved to use her as he would. Not that he wanted to hurt her in any way, but he had the idea of carrying her up to the big house, to show her to the rich folk who lived there. He thought that they might fancy displaying her in their ornamental ponds and be willing to pay a large sum of money for her.

So he ignored her pleas and crying, and rowed back to the bank as fast as he could. All the time, she was struggling to get out of the net that held her, and at last she got one arm completely free. She pointed up to the moon with it, then touched his arm fleetingly. (Afterwards, he said that it felt like she was brushing him with ice-cold foam.) Then she shrank away from him, shivering and shuddering as if she couldn't bear his warmth, and lay down in the bottom of the boat with her long, green hair spread out over her like a blanket.

After that, to his relief, she was still and silent, and he turned his back on her and got on with his rowing, because although the lake wasn't that big, for some reason it was taking him half an age to get back to the shore. By the time he finally made it, the first streaks of dawn were lighting the sky. He hauled the boat up the bank, then leaned over to pull her out – but she wasn't there. Nothing: just a big wet patch in the bottom of the boat with a strange, bittersweet smell to it, showing where she'd been lying.

He swore he hadn't dreamed her. And he swore that the part of his arm where she'd touched him stayed icy cold for the rest of his life.

The Forbidden Forest

· Warwickshire ·

The Forbidden Forest

 king was once riding through his realm, when his eye fell upon a young girl, and he desired to marry her. The poor girl was appalled, for the king was well known to be cruel, and he was also old and repulsive. So without pausing to think, she refused his advances. Of course, the king was furious and tried to take her by force, but the girl was quick and clever enough to distract him, and as soon as his back was turned, she ran away and hid.

When the king realized she had evaded him, his fury knew no bounds. He vowed revenge against all of her kind, sealing every border of his kingdom with high fences and fierce guards. Then he announced:

'From now on, any maiden that takes my fancy is mine. And as soon as I tire of her, I shall kill her.'

And so began a reign of terror. Every day, the king sent his soldiers out to capture a new bride; every night he decapitated the luckless girl with his own sword.

The girl who had rejected him was as terrified as all the rest, for it could only be a matter of time before he tracked her down. Since the sealed border made it impossible for her to flee abroad, her parents sent her away to live with her grandmother, for by good fortune the old woman's cottage stood by a remote forest, where few travellers ever ventured.

For a while, the girl seemed to be safe. She helped her grandmother with her spinning, and once a week, the old woman took the finished hanks of wool to sell in the market. While she was gone, the girl hid in the attic, away from prying eyes.

However, one day her grandmother fell ill.

'I'm not well enough to go to market today,' she groaned. 'But unless I sell some more wool, we shall starve.'

'I'll go instead,' the girl offered. 'It's not very far, the king's never been seen in these parts, and I'm so tired of being shut up in the cottage.'

'That's all very well,' said her grandmother, 'but the king isn't the only danger. There's the forest to fear as well.'

The girl looked at her in astonishment.

'Yes indeed,' said her grandmother, 'even the king has no power over the forest. For it is ruled by a marvellous and very dangerous tree: an oak so ancient that no one can remember how long ago it first sprouted from an acorn. This oak is like no other tree in the whole world, for it has a heart and a mind of its own. It hates people, and will not suffer any human being to pass it. So if you are truly brave enough to risk this errand, my dear, I must warn you to be on your guard against the forest, as well as the king.'

The girl nodded, then took the basket and set off along the road that led to market. But she hadn't gone far before she heard horses pounding along behind her. Turning round, what should she see but a large hunting party – and riding at its head was the king!

What could the poor girl do? She could never outrun the king's horse. It was too late to go back and hide in the cottage. There was only one possible way to escape – and that was to enter the forest.

So the girl took a deep breath and went in.

Soon she was deep inside the forest. There was no sound but that of soft leaf-fall. There was nothing to see but dark trunks and gnarled twigs. She glanced back, but the trees had already closed up behind her: the only path was the one that led ahead.

So she walked on until the path came to a dead end. And there in front of her stood the marvellous oak.

This oak was a like a giant. It was broader than five sturdy men, towering into the sky, massively weighed down by galls and acorns, the wisdom of a thousand summers and winters scarred into its crusty, insect-ridden bark.

When the girl reached it, she dropped a curtsey.

The oak did not move.

But at once a breeze went rustling through the forest, and the path opened up again before her. She continued to walk along it, making for the far edge of the forest and the sunlight, which she could now see, not far ahead. The trees closed ranks behind her, covering her tracks.

Now, although the king too knew all about the dangerous oak, his craving to abuse the girl was stronger than any fear he had of a mere tree. His men cautioned him against entering the forest, of course; but he just roared back at them: 'Nothing in my realm may bar the way to its king!'

So he rode into the forest after the girl. The first trees opened up to let him through, just as they had for her, and very soon he too reached the oak.

For a moment, he paused and stared at it disdainfully; then he spat out an evil curse, and spurred his horse to ride past it.

No sooner had the foul words left his lips, than there came a horrendous cracking noise. A heavy branch broke from the oak as the king passed under it, knocking him off his horse and crushing his neck.

But that's not all. The king's men heard his death cry and rushed into the wood straight after him. Maybe they thought they could still save him, or cut the oak tree down. But the other trees closed in on them at once, filling the forbidden forest with darkness. Neither the evil king, nor any of his followers, was ever seen again.

The King
of England's
Three Sons

· Gypsy ·

The King of England's Three Sons

 here was once a King of England who fell seriously ill. All the doctors said that no medicine could possibly cure him, but that if someone could fetch a dish of enchanted golden apples from a secret garden in a faraway country, that might do the trick. So the king called his three sons to his bedside and commanded them to go on a quest to seek the apples, and not to return until they had found them.

The eldest prince set out first. He rode up hills, down dales and through forests for many days until, just as the sun was setting, he came to a curious tumbledown cottage. Sitting in front of it was a hideous old man with long, yellow teeth like walrus tusks hanging over his lips.

'Welcome, friend!' the hideous old man greeted him. 'Come into my parlour, share a bowl of broth with me, then sleep the night in my spare bed.'

The eldest prince wasn't keen, for the cottage was dingy and dirty, but he was desperate for somewhere to rest, so he accepted the invitation. After a sparse meal, he climbed the narrow staircase to a little bedroom; but no sooner had he blown out his candle and pulled up the covers, than there came a raucous sound of croaking and hissing. The next moment he was assailed by dozens of frogs and snakes, which hopped and writhed from under the floorboards and into his bed.

The eldest prince didn't wait to experience any more! He jumped up and threw off the revolting creatures, then got dressed and rushed straight out of the cottage.

So, *his* adventure ended almost as soon as it had started, and he set off for home empty-handed.

Next, the middle prince set out, came to the same cottage, met the same hideous old man and slept in the bed where the snakes and frogs came creeping. But he was far braver than his elder brother and survived the night's ordeal.

The next day, the old man congratulated him on his robustness. After they had shared a hearty breakfast, he took the middle prince outside and gave him a fresh horse saying, 'Ride forth, young man, and soon you will come to another tumbledown cottage which is the home of my friend – who is even uglier than I am. He will direct you on your way.'

So the middle prince rode on and came to a little house that was barely more than a ruin. Sitting outside it was a truly revolting old fellow whose fingernails and toenails were wound round his neck like a petrified muffler, for they had not been cut for a thousand years. He welcomed the middle prince in, gave him a simple but generous meal and showed him up a broken staircase to a cobwebby bedroom for the night. But no sooner had the middle prince settled down, than mice came scuttling out from behind the skirting boards, and hornets came buzzing in from holes in the rafters. Before he knew it, the middle prince was being bitten and stung all over, but he decided to grin and bear it. The next morning, the revolting old man gave him a fresh horse and, congratulating the middle prince on his steadfastness, sent him on his way to yet another tumbledown cottage.

This one turned out to be a roofless hovel, and the grotesque old man seated in front of it had ears where his nose should have been, and a nose sticking up on top of his head. But he gave the middle prince a tasty dinner then showed him to a very pleasant bedroom, and the middle prince slept right through the night there without any disturbance at all.

The next morning, the grotesque old man said to the middle prince: 'You have done well, young man, to get thus far. Next you must travel on until you reach a large castle surrounded by a wide moat of black water. If you can cross the moat successfully on the back of a swan, evade the monsters who guard the gates, and creep through the castle without waking the princess who lies asleep inside it, you will come at last to the secret garden where the golden apples grow. But take care when you carry them back to your father, and make sure you do not so much as glance behind, not even once; for if you do, your whole journey will prove to be in vain.'

The middle prince thanked him kindly, and then the grotesque old man gave him a fresh horse and sent him on along the road. Soon a magnificent castle with many towers and turrets came into view, surrounded by a wide, black moat. Three swans were roosting on the bank. When he called to them, the largest swan rose, came towards him, and lay down for the middle prince to climb upon its back. Then it carried him safely across the dark water.

The middle prince arrived in front of a portcullis, guarded by two enormous giants with drawn swords, but they were both asleep and he managed to creep past them. Then he came to an iron gate guarded by a sleeping lion, and a wooden gate guarded by slumbering serpents and fire-breathing dragons; but he went past them on tiptoe, and none of the creatures woke to stop him.

Now he was inside the castle. Noticing an open door, he glanced inside the room and saw the most beautiful princess in the whole world, lying fast asleep on a golden bed. But he stifled the temptation to disturb her, and hurried on until he came to the stairs that led down to the castle kitchen. He descended these quickly, passed through the empty kitchen to an outer door and, stepping through this, entered the secret garden where an ancient tree grew, laden with enchanted golden apples.

The middle prince filled his bag to the brim with the golden apples, and then hastened back the way he had come.

But as he rode home with his bounty, he was assailed by a terrible noise of strange voices screaming pitifully: 'Oh prince, please help us!'

'Here we are behind you – can't you see our suffering?'

'If only you would turn round and save us from our misery!'

Remembering the grotesque old man's warning, he blocked his ears and stared resolutely ahead, but he could not escape the voices. On and on they went, tearing at his heartstrings, until he could not help but glance behind.

Of course, when he did, he saw nobody and nothing, and realized that the voices he had heard were from his own imagination. And when he turned back, cursing his own stupidity, he found that his bag was now empty, for the golden apples had vanished.

So that was the end of *his* adventure, and he too returned home empty-handed.

Finally, it was the turn of the youngest prince.

This young man also stayed at the three tumbledown cottages with the hideous, the revolting and the grotesque old men, surviving the night horrors of the first two, and receiving helpful advice before he left the third. He too rode on a fresh horse to the castle, crossed the black moat on a swan's back, passed through the three gates without awakening their slumbering guardians, and made his way to the secret garden, where he picked a big bag of enchanted golden apples.

But unlike the middle prince, he did not pass by the sleeping princess. Instead he crept up to her, gently removed her garter and put it on his own leg, then put his garter on her leg. The princess stirred, sighed and smiled, but she did not waken.

And when the youngest prince was on his way home and the mysterious voices started screaming and groaning behind him, begging him to turn round and help, he hardened his heart and managed not to glance around, not even once, even slightly.

In this way, he arrived at the borders of his kingdom, carrying the bag of golden apples intact, ready to save his father's life.

Now, before the three princes set out on their quest all that time ago, they had agreed that, when all had finished their adventures, they would meet at a particular crossroads before proceeding back together to the palace of their father, the King.

It so happened that the youngest prince arrived before his two elder brothers. Being very weary from his quest, he lay down on the verge, using the bag of golden apples as a pillow, and quickly fell into a deep sleep.

While he was thus lost to the world, his two elder brothers arrived. They saw he had managed to bring back the golden apples where they had both failed, and were consumed by jealousy, for they feared that once the king was cured, he would favour the youngest brother over them. So, working speedily and deviously, they removed the golden apples from under his head and replaced them with a bag of rotten crab apples, sharing the stolen golden apples between themselves.

The youngest prince woke up and greeted his brothers cheerfully, for he had no idea that they had played a malicious trick upon him. Together they went to the palace, entered the King of England's sickroom and presented him with their apples.

The king bit into a golden apple that the eldest prince offered him, and at once the colour returned to his faded cheeks. Then he bit into a golden apple that the middle prince offered him, and straightaway sat up in bed with a smile. But when he bit into the youngest prince's offering – which of course was a rotten crab apple – he immediately began to cough and retch.

'What have you brought me, you wicked boy?' he cried. 'You are trying to poison me! Guards – seize him! Order the executioner to chop off the wretch's head!'

So the youngest prince was hustled away, albeit unjustly, and taken to the executioner. But it so happened that the executioner's wife was with child at the time and couldn't bear to hear the sound of people's heads being chopped off because it gave her a funny turn. For her sake, the executioner led the youngest prince out of earshot and right into the forest to do the horrible deed. On the way to this lonely spot, the youngest prince managed to wriggle out of his manacles and give the executioner the slip.

Meanwhile, in the magnificent castle surrounded by the black moat in the faraway country, the most beautiful princess in the whole world woke up on her golden bed. She saw, to her astonishment, that the delicate lace garter she always wore had been replaced by one that must surely belong to a man. Seeing the heraldic design of a lion and unicorn embroidered on it, she guessed at once that her secret admirer was a prince of the kingdom of England, and was smitten by a desire to meet him. So she summoned her army and led them all the way to England, where she stormed into the king's palace and demanded to know if this strange garter belonged to any of his sons. The eldest prince came in and claimed it was his, but the princess (who was very wise) refused to believe him. Then the middle prince came in and said exactly the same thing.

The very next moment, the youngest prince burst in at a run, trying to dodge the executioner, who was chasing after him with his axe. As he passed by, the princess spotted that her own lacy garter was on his leg and, since he was as handsome as he was nimble, immediately claimed him as her lover.

Before anyone could say anything, the pair had decided to get married and move to the princess's kingdom, for her father had just died and she badly wanted the youngest prince to become the new king. The executioner threw down his axe and offered them his congratulations; the eldest and middle brothers confessed their trick and begged the young couple's forgiveness; and the King of England (who was now completely recovered, thanks to the golden apples) said he had never witnessed such an extraordinary turn of affairs in all his born days, and willingly gave them his blessing.

And that's just about the end of my tale, except to tell you this, my friend: if you believe even half of this fine old nonsense, you're more of a fool than I am!

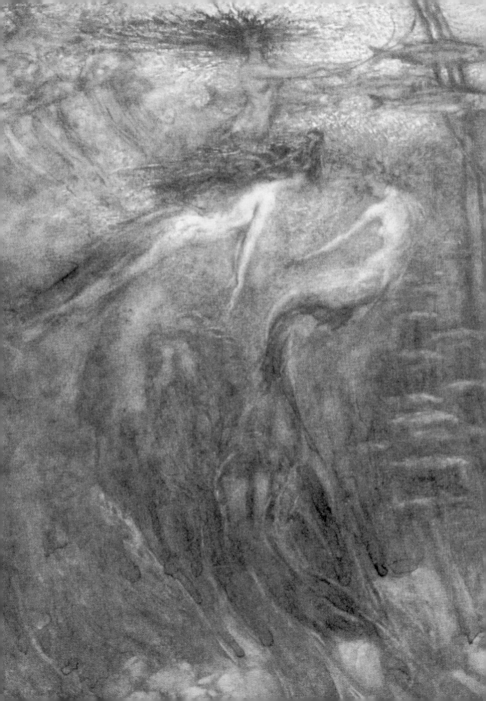

Notes and Sources

Notes and Sources

King Arthur and the Hideous Hag

Armistead: *Tales and Legends of the English Lakes*
Chaucer: *The Canterbury Tales*
Findler: *Legends of the Lake Counties*
Walker: *Folk Stories from the Lake District*
White: *King Arthur in Legend and History*

The story of King Arthur is Britain's greatest legend, first properly recorded in Geoffrey of Monmouth's twelfth-century work, *Historia Regum Britanniae* (History of the Kings of Britain), and then much more comprehensively in English by Sir Thomas Malory in his monumental work *Le Morte d'Arthur* (The Death of Arthur), which was written in the mid-fifteenth century. This tells how Arthur, fostered from infancy and not realizing he is the rightful heir to King Uther Pendragon, his real father, gains the throne in his youth by pulling a magical sword from a stone. Guided by the mysterious Wizard Merlin, he unites the warring petty kingdoms of Britain and rules over them in peace, plenitude and glory, aided by his valiant Knights of the Round Table. This golden age finally comes to an end with the revelation that his wife, Queen Guinevere, is conducting an adulterous love affair with one of his leading knights, Sir Lancelot, causing the kingdom to split asunder.

Over the centuries, there has been much scholarly debate about whether Arthur actually existed. Today, some historians believe that the 'real' Arthur was probably not a king but a great fifth-century Christian warrior who, following the Roman withdrawal from Britain, led the native British people to victory in a number of battles against pagan Anglo-Saxon invaders. His name is cryptically mentioned in several Dark Age manuscripts.

In the Middle Ages, the legend of King Arthur became famous throughout Britain and in many European countries, particularly France (where Chrétien de Troyes was the first to write down many important Arthurian romances), Germany, Italy, the Netherlands, Portugal, Scandinavia and Spain; and many other fantastical tales were woven into the grand tapestry of the main story. *King Arthur and the Hideous Hag* is one of them.

Perhaps the oldest and best-known version of the story is 'The Wife of Bath's Tale' from *The Canterbury Tales* by Geoffrey Chaucer (late fourteenth century). Here, an unnamed knight rapes a damsel and is sentenced to death, but the queen agrees to spare him if he can answer a riddle: 'What thyng is it that women moost desiren?' The motif is echoed in *The Wedding of Sir Gawen and Dame Ragnell* (c.1450), which locates the tale in Inglewood, in modern Cumbria. Arthur, out hunting in the forest, is threatened by a knight bent on revenge because Arthur has gifted that knight's lands to Sir Gawain. The knight agrees to spare Arthur's life if he returns, alone, in exactly a year with the answer to the riddle 'Whate wemen love best in feld and town'. Arthur meets an ugly old hag, Dame Ragnell, who gives the answer in return for being married to Sir Gawain, resulting in her transformation.

Armistead, writing in 1891, quotes an old ballad, *The Marriage of Sir Gawaine*. Here, King Arthur's castle is firmly placed in Carlisle, where the royal Christmas feast is interrupted by 'a faire damsel' who begs a 'boone' of Arthur: to take revenge on an evil knight, the 'grimme barone', who is 'twice the size of common men' and who has 'bare my love and sore misused me'. Arthur's attempt to punish the knight results in the supernatural paralysis of his sword arm, from which he can only be freed by solving the same riddle. The hag tells him the answer on condition that he brings her 'a fair courtly knight to marry her', and Sir Gawain boldly volunteers for the task. But there is another twist here: after she transforms into a 'young ladye faire', she asks Sir Gawain to choose whether he would prefer her in her 'fair' form by day or by night, as to have both is not possible. After some deliberation, he defers and allows her to 'have all thy wille' – thus putting the riddle's answer to good practical use and breaking the malevolent spell completely.

Walker, in recounting the same tale, says that Inglewood Forest, where the Cumbrian version is set, was once huge. Within it there was previously a small lake, now drained, called Tarn Wadlyn; on its shores stood Castle Hewin, which has now disappeared, but which was a well-known ruin in the sixteenth century, with walls up to eight feet thick – the supposed home of the giant of the story.

Sir Gawain was one of King Arthur's most prominent knights, and also the king's nephew: he was the son of King Lot of Lothian and Orkney, and one of King Arthur's sisters. The main Arthurian romances depict him as a bold yet courteous warrior-knight, a friend and confidant of the king. The most famous story about him in Old English is the ballad of *Sir Gawain and the Green Knight* (c.1400), in which a giant, clad in green, enters the court and challenges any knight to strike him with an axe and then be struck in return. Gawain volunteers and cuts off the Green Knight's head, but the Green Knight casually picks it up and rides off, commanding Sir Gawain to meet him a year later at the Green Chapel (said to be in the Wirral, Cheshire) and rides away.

As the year ends, Gawain travels there to meet his fate, staying en route at a castle where he gallantly resists the amorous temptations of the lord's wife. It turns out that the Green Knight is in fact the lord of that castle, and he spares Gawain's life as a reward for passing his wife's test.

King Arthur and the Hideous Hag contains many elements typical of Arthurian romance. It opens at a feast on a special day in the calendar, with the king eagerly seizing the chance of adventure. In some stories he actually forbids such a feast to begin until he has witnessed some 'marvel'. The tableau of someone bursting into the royal castle to make a dramatic plea or challenge is another common feature.

Magic appears in many strands of Arthurian legend. A famous episode tells how King Arthur's evil sister, Morgan le Fay, sends Arthur a bewitched cloak, which bursts into flames when someone puts it on. Like the hag, Morgan can change shape: at one stage she appears as a deer to lead Arthur astray, and just before the king is mortally wounded in his last battle, she transforms into a snake. Many Arthurian stories are enriched by enchantment: expeditions into the forest lead to strange places and encounters, weapons have supernatural powers, and even where Christianity enters the frame, as in the quest for the Holy Grail, it is laden with mysticism.

King Arthur and the Hideous Hag locates King Arthur's castle at Carlisle in Cumbria, but more commonly it was supposed to be at 'Camelot', which some archaeologists believe may have been the 5,000-year-old hill fort at Cadbury in Somerset. Local folklore claims that King Arthur and his knights are still sleeping inside the fort, waiting to be awoken when England needs them again. Similar legends are associated with Richmond Castle in North Yorkshire, Merbach Hill near Dorstone, Herefordshire, and the ruined Sewingshields Castle in Northumberland.

Many other English locations have strong associations with the legend. Tintagel Castle in Cornwall is said to be the place where King Arthur was conceived and born, after Wizard Merlin had transformed his father, King Uther Pendragon, into the shape of Gorlois, Earl of Cornwall, in order to illicitly make love to the earl's wife, Igraine. Merlin himself is said to have made his home at Alderley Edge in Cheshire. Badbury Rings, an Iron Age hill fort in Dorset, is said to be the site of the Battle of Badon, which the historical hero Arthur fought and won, bringing twenty-one years of peace. Bamburgh Castle in Northumberland is reputedly built on the site of Sir Lancelot's castle, Joyous Gard. Glastonbury in Somerset is claimed to be the mythical Isle of Avalon, where King Arthur was taken to be healed after being mortally wounded in his last battle. Here, too, is supposedly the place where King Arthur and Queen Guinevere are buried.

Tom Tit Tot

Briggs: *A Dictionary of British Folk-Tales*
Jacobs: *English Fairy Tales*

Although Tom Tit Tot is destroyed at the end of his story, what happens to the king's foolish wife is left in the air – for the king, if you remember, had ordained that she must spend the last month of every year spinning for the rest of her life. Briggs quotes a traditional dialect ending that goes: 'Lork! How she did clap her hands for joy. "I'll warrant my master'll ha' forgot all about the spinning next year," says she.' Briggs also gives another Suffolk story, *The Gypsy Woman*, which provides a clever and satisfying sequel: The following year, shortly before the girl is due to be locked in the tower with the spinning wheel again, a gypsy woman comes to the door and

offers to help in return for the girl's best clothes and jewels, which are
gladly given. The gypsy tells the girl to throw a big party at the palace,
which the gypsy attends incognito, magnificently dressed in the girl's
clothes. As the guests play blind man's buff, the gypsy seizes the chance to
smear many of the ladies' dresses with grease, and an argument breaks out
over who is responsible. The gypsy confesses to the king, explaining that
the grease is permanently ingrained in her fingers from spinning five
skeins every day. She warns that the girl's fingers will become similarly
greasy and ruined if she too spins at that rate – so the king hastily forbids
her ever to spin again!

'Magic helpers' are an essential ingredient of many traditional stories
throughout the world. Often their help is given freely and unconditionally,
as by the fairy godmother in the French *Cinderella* story, whose role is
echoed in England by the gooseherd in *Tattercoats* and the hen-wife in
Catskin. But some helpers set a task or test before bestowing their
benevolent gifts. A strange Lincolnshire story, *Sorrow and Love*, follows a
girl's quest to find the lover who bit off her finger. Her helper is a
mysterious old woman who asks her to weep a bowl full of tears, then in
return gives her a magic pear which makes wonderful music when cut and
enables her to get into her lover's castle. In *The Three Heads of the Well*,
known throughout England, a princess, banished by a heartless
stepmother, is generous to two sets of potential helpers: firstly an old man
with whom she shares her meagre rations, then three supernatural 'golden
heads' that appear from a well asking her to wash and comb them. She is
rewarded with extra beauty, good fortune and marriage to a king. Her
stepsister callously tries to emulate her but refuses to do anything for her
potential benefactors, and so is cursed into poverty. This pattern of
'kindness rewarded, wickedness punished' is a very widespread theme.

Tom Tit Tot is a helper of a different kind: seemingly generous yet really deceitful and curmudgeonly, using his help as a malicious trap. There are many similar stories from around Europe. The best known is probably the German *Rumpelstiltskin*, collected by the Brothers Grimm, which has a very similar opening, although here the simpleton girl's father boasts that she can spin straw into gold. The king orders her to perform this feat three times, and on each occasion she is helped by a little dwarf who claims first her necklace, then her ring, and then finally her first child. When the baby is born a year later and the dwarf comes to claim it, he offers her an escape if she can guess his name – which one of her messengers happens to overhear him chanting. A Scottish version, *Whuppity Stoorie*, also features the helper claiming the victim's baby unless she can correctly guess the name.

There are two charming variants, both told in Cornwall. In *Duffy and the Devils*, the girl's helper is called Terrytop, and goes up in smoke at the end. More unusually, *Foul-Weather* is the secret name of a gnome who helps the king 'of a far country' to build a cathedral, threatening to steal the king's heart for his gnome-baby to play with unless the king can guess the name. In all these stories, the name is discovered purely by chance, but in a straightforward manner.

The idea of a secret or taboo name has its roots in ancient beliefs shared by many cultures. In Ancient Egypt, the name was identified with the immortal soul and it was thus particularly dangerous to be cursed by name. In witchcraft lore, simply speaking the name of an evil spirit was enough to conjure it up. In Egypt, Babylon and India, to name a god was to compel him to answer a prayer. Imperial China made it a crime to use the real name of the reigning emperor. At the other end of the scale, many cultures used euphemisms to avoid naming feared animals: Siberian bears were called 'little old man' or 'grandfather', whilst Sumatrans called the tiger 'he with a striped coat'. This background is echoed in the desire to avoid calling fairies by the actual word, and helps make sense of Tom Tit Tot's anxiety about keeping his own name secret. It adds to his outrageousness that he breaks the taboo by shouting his name out loud when he thinks he cannot be overheard.

The Dead Moon
Briggs: *A Dictionary of British Folk-Tales*

Goblins, bogies, bogles, bugs or bug-a-boos: the unsavoury creatures of this story, sometimes described as nature spirits, seem to be a species halfway between fairies and ghosts. Tales and rumours of their kind, either solitary or in a group, were once common in the bleak and swampy fen country or 'cars' of Lincolnshire. Here they were often called tiddy ones, tiddy people or yarthkins. They haunted the bogs, crying out with the voices of dead people (possibly really the mournful cries of wading birds), enticing passers-by to stray from the path, trying to clutch at them with outstretched hands, and mingling with witches and the flickering lights of will-o'-tha-wykes (will-o'-the-wisps). Two things were liable to make them particularly dangerous: the draining of the fens where they lived, and failure to pay the 'tribute' they claimed.

The most famous of these bogles was the Tiddy Mun himself – a little brute of a man with long, tangly white hair and beard and a grey gown, who inhabited slimy green waterholes. One local story told of a time when some of the fens were being drained, and the Tiddy Mun took revenge by dragging many of the men working there into the bog, and causing cows, pigs and children to fall ill and die, and houses to collapse. Luckily, he was readily placated when his human neighbours poured an offering of fresh water into the edge of his territory.

There were will-o'-the-wisps in the West Country too, but here they were one-legged and went by the name of hinky-punks. However, the commonest danger in those parts was from the wish hounds, yell hounds, yeth hounds or Devil's dandy dogs – a pack of spectral dogs (sometimes headless, sometime snorting fire and yelping) believed to go hunting with the Devil. Related to these was the Wild Hunt, a pack of ghostly dogs accompanied by men and horses, all dark as night with ghastly, staring eyes.

Some fishermen dreaded the seven whistlers – weird spirits who were a portent of death when they came soaring suddenly overhead with mournful cries. A Kent anecdote recalled one occasion when this happened: the whistlers were quickly followed by a violent rainstorm in which a boat overturned and seven men were drowned. Up in Lancashire, a similar phenomenon was known as gabriel hounds, gabriel ratchets or sky yelpers – ghostly beings with canine bodies and human heads who flew high through the air, screeching and beating their wings.

In the North East, the terror was of brags: tricksterish, shape-shifting spirits who might appear as a horse, a calf or even a headless, naked man. A particularly malicious form of this was the Northumbrian dunnie, whose favourite jape was to transform itself into the family horse whenever the midwife was needed, and then toss both the new father and the midwife into a stream.

Nasty as these creatures were, it was fairly easy to get the better of them with a bit of quick thinking and cunning. One Northamptonshire farmer apparently had a field taken over by a bogie, who ordered the following arrangement: the farmer would do all the work, but the produce would be split between them, with the farmer allowed to harvest only 'the top' (i.e. the crop above ground) and the bogie taking 'the bottom' (the crop below the ground). The farmer, realizing that the bogie was as stupid as he was evil, planted wheat, so that he got all the grain while the bogie got only stubble. The following year the bogie insisted on reversing the deal, so the farmer planted turnips: taking the bottom for himself, he had a good crop of root vegetables, while the bogie got only useless leaves. In the third year, the bogie insisted on a ploughing match, with the winner taking the entire crop, but the farmer sabotaged the bogie's half of the field with iron rods, so the ill-tempered brute gave up and vanished.

A Yorkshire story recounts how a man stumbled upon a dancing troupe of evil goblins, witches and boggarts. He hastily averted his eyes, knowing that this precaution should keep him out of trouble, but he couldn't stop himself sneezing. At once the goblins leaped at him – but he escaped them by jumping into a nearby well that was dedicated to 'Our Lady' and justly reputed to be a safe place to hide from supernatural beings. For there was one reassuring thing about all these evil spirits: they had no power over anything sacred, be it a whispered prayer, a holy building, a lucky charm or even a crumpled page torn from a Bible.

Jack the Giant-Killer

Briggs: *A Dictionary of British Folk-Tales*
Jacobs: *English Fairy Tales*

There are several versions of this tale: storytellers of old would have expanded freely on earlier forms and added their own episodes. The one here is based largely on the form that Briggs sourced from a nineteenth-century book by E. S. Hartland, called *English Fairy and Folk Tales*; she also gives a somewhat nonsensical alternative version from Herefordshire. Jacobs found the story in two chapbooks (small pamphlets sold by pedlars) in the British Museum, dated 1805 and 1814. Interestingly, the incident in which Jack tricks a giant into cutting open his own stomach is almost identical to one recounted in a Norwegian folk tale about a boy captured by a troll.

If the old storytellers can be believed, England was once riddled with giants, from the north country to Cornwall, and many familiar landmarks are the result of their activities. One of the best-known stories is about a hill in Shropshire called the Wrekin. The tale goes that a local giant, who had fallen out with the good citizens of Shrewsbury, was carrying an enormous spade of earth with which he intended to flood the River Severn where it flowed through the town. But on the way he got lost and asked directions from a passing cobbler. The cobbler, guessing the giant's evil intentions, tricked him by pointing to all the broken shoes he was carrying and saying, 'Look, I've come from Shrewsbury myself, and it's such a long way that I've worn out all these shoes on my journey!' The stupid giant decided to give up and despondently dumped all the earth on the spot – which is how the Wrekin came to be.

Similarly, in Somerset, it is claimed that the long earthwork of Wansdyke was dropped on the land by the clumsy Giant Gorm. He was chased into the sea by the Lord of Avon, fell over his own feet and drowned: the remains of his body became the two islands of Steep Holm and Flat Holm. In Yorkshire, Giant Wade and Giantess Bell were credited with building the castles of Mulgrave and Pickering, the Roman road between them, and several local 'druid stones'. A pair of Cornish giants, Giant Cormoron and Giantess Cormelian, were supposedly responsible for the causeway to St Michael's Mount. And in Dorset, the huge chalk figure cut into the hill at Cerne Abbas is said to be the mark left by an invading

Danish giant who lay down to sleep, but was tied down by locals and had his head cut off.

The existence of giantesses as well as giants suggests that the English breed evolved from the frost giants of Norse mythology, for these too were represented by both sexes. The Norse giants – who were at constant war with the gods – lived beyond the ocean in the bleak, stormy, frozen lands of Jotunheim or Giant Land, but sometimes trespassed into the human world where they made trouble. Many of the giantesses were as beautiful as they were big, but their menfolk could be brutish and either stupid or maliciously cunning – traits which they passed on to their English descendants.

For example, in County Durham, two evil giants were once the bane of Weardale. Yorkshire was terrorized by the Giant of Penhill, who had an unsavoury taste for the flocks of sheep and maidens of Wensleydale, and by the one-eyed giant of Dalton Mill near Thirsk, who ground human bones to make his bread. In Somerset, a whole gang of giants built a mound castle at Nether Stowey, from which they only had to reach out to grab any sheep, cow or person who took their fancy. But luckily, these brutes were neither immortal nor indestructible. An aggressive Hampshire giant called Ascapart was slain by one Sir Bevis. A murderous, head-hunting giant in Wisbech, Cambridgeshire, was defeated by a hero called Tom Hickathrift, who was almost of gigantic size himself. In Cornwall, another cattle-stealing giant from St Michael's Mount was outwitted by the legendary Lord of Pengerswick, who worked witchcraft to paralyse him, then chained him to a rock over a precipice and gave him such a whipping that he never dared trouble the mainland again. A Hertfordshire cave-dwelling giant, Jack o' Legs, who like Robin Hood robbed the rich to feed the poor, was caught and bound by his victims, who allowed him to fire one last arrow before they finished him off: the arrow flew three miles and fell at Weston, which became the site of the creature's grave.

Nevertheless, some giants were more decent fellows, and were often associated with treasure. Two Shropshire giants left a hoard of treasure in a vault below Stokesay Castle, though no one can ever retrieve it since they lost the key in the castle moat, and besides it is guarded by a hostile raven. Another giant's treasure is hidden in the earth at Addleborough, Yorkshire: anyone who wishes to excavate it must first be lucky enough to come across the giant who, confusingly, will be disguised in the shape of a hen or an ape. The treasure must then be dug out in utter silence, for if the finder gives even a cry of joy when he sees it, he will lose it forever.

Among the benevolent giants were one who lived at Grabbist in Somerset who, it is said, rescued a boat from a storm and also fought the Devil. The giant of Carn Galva in Cornwall was a playful fellow, and it was purely an accident when he killed his human friend by tapping his head with his gigantic fingertips. Another Cornish giant was big-hearted enough to forgive the youth who broke into his castle and gored him to death: the good giant's dying act was to leave both castle and treasure to his apologetic murderer.

So, where have all the giants gone today? In County Durham, three friendly giants, Cor, Ben and Con, who used the hills above Consett as their smithies, fell victim to an ancient curse. Their habit was to share their tools by throwing them to each other, even though they knew that if any of them failed to catch an implement, the giants would all vanish. In old age, Con became blind and missed his catch, so that was the end of them. Meanwhile, Giant Bolster, who lived on Dartmoor in Devon, courted St Agnes of Cornwall and was tricked by her into proving his love by filling a bottomless well with his blood, killing himself in the process. His good friend, a giant called Gogmagog, who had recently returned from the Trojan wars, was so upset by this that he lay down on the moors. There the Trojans themselves found him and dragged him out to sea to drown. It is said that this frightened off all the remaining giants, who fled across the English Channel – and then died out from homesickness.

'Jack' is the archetypal English folk-tale hero. Of humble birth, he often begins life as an ash-lad, an idle ne'er-do-well, too fond of his own mother and of lazing around the fire. Forced out into the world to seek his fortune, he overcomes his idleness and stupidity, and often ends up with a pile of treasure and sometimes even a royal bride.

The best-known 'Jack' story is the pantomime favourite, *Jack and the Beanstalk*, which pitches the hero firmly against a giant. Jack's mother sends him to market with some goods to sell, but the foolish boy is duped and returns home with nothing more than a handful of beans in his pocket. He scatters these in the garden and overnight they grow into an enormous plant that extends into the clouds. Jack climbs the plant and finds himself in the castle of a ferocious, man-eating giant. The giant's wife helps him escape with a bag of gold, a golden harp and a hen that lays golden eggs, and when the giant pursues him, Jack cuts down the beanstalk, sending the giant crashing to his death. In an alternative version, Jack, on reaching the top of the beanstalk, is helped by a fairy. She reveals that Jack's father was murdered by a giant who also stole Jack's rightful inheritance. The tale then proceeds as above. There is also a gypsy version in which the giant is absent and both treasure and castle belong to an old woman who lives at the top of the beanstalk.

A story called *How Jack Went to Seek his Fortune* carries strong echoes of a well-known German folk tale, *The Musicians of Bremen*. In the story Jack, making his way through the world for the first time, meets a cat, a dog, a goat, a bull and a rooster who all volunteer to accompany him. This unusual band frightens away a gang of robbers and is rewarded by a share-out of the loot.

In *Jack and the Buttermilk*, the hero refuses to give a wicked witch a taste of his buttermilk, so she throws him into a bag and threatens to boil him alive; but it turns out that he is a talented trickster, and manages to escape. A rather gruesome Yorkshire version also makes Jack good at tricks: when Jack is caught and enslaved by the one-eyed Giant of Dalton Mill mentioned above, he gouges out the eye with the giant's own bread knife, then kills the brute's dog, dresses in its skin and in this disguise escapes by running straight through the enraged and blinded giant's legs.

Lazy Jack, or *Jack's Rewards and What He Did With Them*, once popular in Cumbria, shows the anti-hero at his comic best. Jack attempts a series of casual jobs for which he is paid in kind, but despite his mother's good advice, he is too stupid to bring the various payments home without losing them. Eventually, still trying to puzzle out his mother's instructions, he stumbles home with a donkey balanced precariously on his shoulder. He is spotted en route by a rich girl, who bursts out laughing at the ridiculous sight, thus curing herself of long-term depression – and as a reward Jack wins her hand in marriage.

Also in Cumbria, we meet another simpleton Jack, whose brothers want to get rid of him. They claim that they are going to travel to heaven in a sack and, as anticipated, he wishes to copy them. They put Jack in a sack and set out to throw him into a river, but on the way stop at an inn. There, another halfwit, on hearing that Jack is bound for heaven, eagerly swaps places with him. Jack sets off for home with the sheep that the halfwit had been driving along the road, and his brothers unknowingly drown the wrong man. They are astonished to return home and find Jack there with his newly acquired sheep, which he claims to have found on the riverbed. It turns out that Jack is not such a fool after all, for he succeeds in tricking his brothers into jumping into the water, hoping to find some sheep for themselves. Inevitably they drown, leaving Jack as sole inheritor of the family farm.

Dragon Castle

Grice: *Folk Tales of the North Country*
Henderson: *Notes on the Folk-Lore of the Northern Counties of England and the Borders*
Service: *Metrical Legends of Northumberland*
Leighton: *Wilson's Tales of the Borders and of Scotland*

This story, commonly known by its old name, *The Laidley Worm of Spindlestone Haugh*, is based on an old ballad, dating from either the eighteenth or thirteenth century, or possibly even from Anglo-Saxon times, depending on which source one believes.

It contains many typical fairy-tale motifs – a wicked stepmother and the bewitching of the innocent heroine into a different shape; she is then rescued by a hero whom she marries. However, in one aspect it is strikingly different: a dragon is usually an evil beast with a predilection for consuming nubile young virgins, rather than being a transformation of one. This shape-shifting element is unusual in Europe, and curiously echoes the benevolent dragon-kings and dragon-princesses of China, Japan and Korea, which change shape between dragon and human form by swallowing a pearl.

Dragons are often called 'worms' – from the old Norse word, *ormr* – and their supposed existence once haunted England. A historical record from 1233 states that dragons were seen fighting in the sky off the south coast, and 160 years later it is recorded that a fierce dragon terrorized many parts of the country. St Leonard's Forest near Horsham, Sussex, was said to have been troubled by a dragon in the sixth century, which was slaughtered by the saint who gave the place its name; as recently as the nineteenth century, local people still claimed that the forest was blighted by these mythical beasts. In 1405, a crested dragon was spotted close to Bures in Suffolk: the local lord sent his workmen to shoot at it with bows and arrows, which just bounced off its thick hide, and the beast finally fled to hide in a marsh. Dragon's blood and dragon's fat were often demanded as ingredients in medieval medicines, and bestiary writers of the time commonly presented them as real-life creatures.

The most famous and symbolic English dragon story is, of course, *St George and the Dragon*, though few English people today would claim to know any details of its plot. A well-developed version describes St George as the son of the Earl of Coventry, High Steward of England. His mother dies at his birth and he is stolen by a wicked, cannibalistic enchantress called Kalyb. Discovering the baby's body to be marked by significant symbols, she spares his life. When he grows up, she falls in love with him, but he seizes her magic wand and imprisons her within a rock. George travels to Egypt, where he finds the land has been laid waste by a dragon who has already devoured all the maidens except for the king's daughter; George slays the dragon and rescues her just in time. However, before he can marry the princess, she is claimed by the King of Morocco, who sends George to the King of Persia with a letter ordering George's execution. George is thus thrown into a den of lions, but he manages to kill them and escape. He returns to Egypt just in time to save the princess from her marriage to his rival, then conquers the three kingdoms of Egypt, Morocco and Persia. Finally, he returns home with his wife to Coventry, where they raise three sons.

The story seems to be inspired by the Crusades, for it is full of references to religious rivalry. However, the 'original' St George is believed to have been a Christian soldier or nobleman from the eastern outposts of the

Roman Empire in the late third century. When Christianity was outlawed on the pretext that it was destroying discipline in the Roman army, George tore down and destroyed the emperor's decree and was martyred as a result. His evolution from Christian martyr to chivalric hero is perhaps less extraordinary when we learn that Christian folklore commonly portrayed the Devil in the disguise of a dragon.

Several English locations claim to be the site where the dragon was slain by St George, including Lower Stanks Field in Brinsop, Herefordshire; Dragon Hill, near the White Horse of Uffingham in Berkshire (where a bare patch in the grass was supposedly caused by the dragon's blood); and St Michael's Mount in Cornwall.

Another famous dragon story, from County Durham, is *The Lambton Worm*. The wayward young heir to Lambton Hall, breaking the sabbath by going fishing, hauls up a dragon from the River Wear. It ravages the surrounding countryside, and in repentance the youth goes to the Holy Land for seven years. On his return, a wise woman advises him to kill the dragon by goring it with the spikes of a specially made suit of armour; he must then kill the first creature he meets on returning home to avoid the dragon's curse. The youth is victorious, so goes home expecting that the first creature he meets there will be his dog – but in the event it is his own elderly father who comes to the door to greet him. Unable to commit patricide, the youth cannot prevent the curse descending upon his family. As a result, nine successive generations of Lambtons die violent deaths.

An interesting part of this tale is the hero's special dragon-killing armour, a motif repeated in a story from Lancashire. Here a knight called More of More Hall dons armour covered in six-inch iron spikes to vanquish a fire-breathing, child-eating dragon: his battle lasts for two whole days and nights. Similarly, a Yorkshire warrior covers his armour in razorblades for his own dragon battle: he destroys and dismembers the beast bit by bit, aided by his faithful dog, who carries the gruesome dragon parts away. However, when the dog returns to lick his triumphant master, it fatally infects him with dragon poison; then the dog too dies, of grief.

But there are less dangerous, more cunning ways to get rid of dragons. A Somerset hero rolls a huge rock on top of one; a Northumberland warrior removes another from the life-giving well where it keeps its tail permanently submerged; some Cumbrian fishermen destroy a dragon that emerges from the sea by goring it on a hundred wooden stakes; and a Sussex youth destroys the 'Knucker' dragon of a bottomless pond by feeding it a poisoned pie.

Norse mythology associates dragons with treasure hoards, as in the Anglo-Saxon poem *Beowulf* and the Norse myth *Sigurd and the Dragon*. Briggs quotes a gypsy woman who described a wingless, creeping, fire-breathing dragon that concealed itself in the mud of Bedfordshire: after it had been killed, its bed was found to comprise a huge heap of treasure.

Robin Hood and the Golden Arrow

Alexander: *British Folklore, Myths and Legends*
Dobson and Taylor: *Rymes of Robyn Hood*
Holt: *Robin Hood*

Robin Hood is the quintessential medieval English hero: outlaw, archer and sword-fighter, admired for his rebellious spirit, his consummate fighting skills and for stealing from the rich to give to the poor. There is no historical proof that such a man ever lived, yet his existence is deeply ingrained in the national consciousness.

The legend's origins go back to at least the fourteenth century. The earliest surviving written reference to it is found in a Middle English poem, *Piers Plowman* by William Langland, which includes the phrase: '*I kan rymes of Robyn hood*'. During the next hundred years the story became a familiar ingredient of ballads, dramas and May Day 'games'.

A manuscript from c.1450 includes a poem called *Talkyng of the Munke and Robyn Hode*. In the late fifteenth to mid-sixteenth centuries, the newly burgeoning printing presses of England and Antwerp produced at least five editions of a lengthy ballad about the heroic outlaw, known as either *A Gest of Robyn Hode* or *A Lyttell Geste of Robyn Hode*. The retelling here is derived from these. Robin Hood has continued to capture popular imagination to the present day, with numerous storytellers, ballad-makers, novelists and film-makers developing, reinterpreting and adding to the original legend.

Robin Hood was said to have lived in the twelfth or thirteenth century: many of the tales place him within the reign of the crusading King Richard I – 'The Lionheart' – to whom Robin was unwaveringly loyal as a representative of true Christian justice. However, *A Gest of Robyn Hode* names his monarch as 'Edwarde our comly kynge'. The earliest sources described Robin as a small farmer, but he was later claimed to be a disinherited nobleman, or a 'native' Englishman resisting Norman domination, or a social rebel defending the peasants against avaricious landowners. Most stories about him are set in South Yorkshire, particularly Barnsdale; also in Nottinghamshire, particularly Sherwood Forest and the city of Nottingham. There are also links with West Yorkshire and Lancashire.

Robin Hood is not a single legend but a cycle of numerous independent tales about Robin's adventures with a motley band of outlaws (sometimes called the Merry Men) who live in hiding in the forest, poach the king's deer and dress in bright green woollen cloth known as Lincoln Green. The best-known outlaws are Little John, a tall, strapping man originally called John Little, and Friar Tuck, a fat, jolly priest. Others include Will Scarlet, Much the Miller's Son, Allen-a-Dale and George-a-Green. The only significant woman is Maid Marian, Robin's sweetheart or wife. The daughter of a nobleman, she escapes an unwanted betrothal by fleeing to the forest disguised as a page. In this guise, she successfully takes part in a sword-fight against the incognito Robin, who then invites her to join his merry band of outlaws.

The theme of the cycle is essentially good against evil, but unlike *King Arthur* there is no central plot to the legend, and no beginning or explanation of how Robin came to be an outlaw living in the forest, although there is a story about Robin's final betrayal and death. Each story features Robin clashing with an enemy: the tales are usually exciting, sometimes amusing and always entertaining, crammed with violent sword-fights and ambushes in which many villains are killed. Some of Robin's enemies survive the violence, change sides and become his allies or even join the outlaws, but not so his arch-enemy, the callous and greedy Sheriff of Nottingham, hated by Robin for his blatant abuse of power. In many of the tales he tries to kill Robin, but is always outwitted.

The theme of an archery contest, as in *Robin Hood and the Golden Arrow*, is a common motif in the cycle. In another example, Robin's adversary appears to be an abbot, but is actually the king himself in disguise, newly returned from abroad. The king is so impressed by Robin's archery skills and by the feast Robin invites him to share, that he officially pardons him for all his crimes. In another commonly reworked plot, Robin encounters a stranger and challenges him to pay a fee, to perform a service, or to show what goods he is carrying. When the stranger refuses to submit, a fight breaks out. Robin is not always the victor: often the stranger turns out to have admirable fighting skills, and Robin is so impressed that he invites the man to join his band of outlaws – an invitation that is usually accepted.

Another common plot sees Robin or one of his men betrayed and captured. Rescue is usually achieved by one of the other principal outlaws, often Little John or even Robin himself, who puts on a disguise that enables him to enter the heart of enemy territory. There is usually at least one violent battle and several deaths before the captured outlaw is freed and reunited with his comrades in the forest. There are also many tales of corrupt, bullying priests and bishops, whom Robin and his men trick, rob or ransom to teach them a lesson.

The final story of the cycle has rather a different tone. Robin is ill and goes to visit his cousin, a prioress who is a renowned healer. She lets his blood – a common medieval healing practice – but has been bribed by an enemy called Red Roger to bleed Robin to death. Little John, who accompanies Robin to the healer, kills Roger, but he is too late to save Robin Hood. In a final act of generosity, Robin forgives his cousin and commands Little John to take him to his grave.

The Weardale Fairies
Grice: *Folk Tales of the North Country*

Fairies are known throughout Europe, but the British Isles surely has one of the richest hoards of stories about them. Briggs's *Dictionary of British Folk-Tales* lists 235 variants, with very similar themes repeated in the stories of England, Scotland and Wales.

Many English regions have their own name for fairies: they are brownies in northern and eastern England, colepexies in Dorset, derricks in Devon and Hampshire, dobbies in Yorkshire and Lancashire, farisees in Suffolk, pixies in Somerset, Devon and Cornwall, and so on. But in earlier times, the use of these names was thought to bring bad luck: it was safer to refer to fairies euphemistically as 'the little people', 'the hill folk', 'the gentry', 'the strangers' or – in the Isle of Man – as 'themselves' or 'them that's in'. 'Elves' is another generic name for fairies, originating in Norse mythology.

Today it is only young children who are assumed to be interested in fairies, but until comparatively recently, adults in country areas also believed in them. Keightley, writing in the late nineteenth century, cites people in Cumbria, Devon, Durham, Hampshire, Norfolk, Northumberland, Suffolk and Yorkshire who claimed they had actually seen fairies.

So what are fairies? They are usually diminutive (though not always), immortal and have wide-ranging supernatural powers, particularly the ability to turn invisible, fly and transform humble objects into treasure. They are cunning, tricksy, dangerous and often malevolent. There are fairies of both sexes, and they generally fall into two types.

The 'trooping' or dancing fairies live communally and are supposedly found revelling in lonely places at twilight, midnight or at special times of year, such as the summer solstice. Their musicians play on pipe, fiddle and drum, and their dances are fast and mesmerizing: ordinary mortals who dare to join in risk being spirited away to a secret world inside the hills or deep underground.

House fairies, on the other hand, are solitary – usually wizened and bearded little old men, who take up residence in the nooks and crannies of ancient farmhouses and other rural buildings. They tend to be more benevolent than trooping fairies and take it upon themselves to help with domestic tasks, but they are also cunning and temperamental, and easily take offence. In return for their help, house fairies expect a regular supply of homely food such as milk, potatoes and porridge; but it is unwise to offer them riches and especially to spy on them, for that will encourage them to abandon their chores and vanish. It is notoriously difficult to get rid of a house fairy. An oft-repeated Yorkshire tale tells of a farming family troubled by a house fairy, or boggart, who constantly played malicious tricks such as hiding things away. In the end they upped and moved house to escape him – only to find that the boggart had moved with them!

What do fairies look like? In size they range from insect-like to the height of a full-grown man, but most commonly they are a similar size to a smallish human three-year-old. Their clothes are naturally old-fashioned, usually coloured green and/or red, though brownies dress to match their name. They usually wear coloured caps, but contrary to modern popular opinion, they rarely sport wings.

Nevertheless, fairies can fly – usually by riding a twig, a stem of ragwort or a bundle of grass, but sometimes by donning a special magic cap. In order to take off, some fairies must recite a simple, nonsensical spell such as 'Hupp, Horse and Handocks!' It is possible for an ordinary mortal to travel with them by borrowing a fairy's magic cap and repeating their charms.

Fairies can be dangerous and inflict cruel punishments on mortals; they also commonly abduct people, especially young women, children and babies. One of the commonest stories is the 'changeling' type, in which the fairies steal an unchristened human infant and substitute one of their own. The changeling baby is usually ill-favoured, ill-tempered, fails to thrive or grow, and comes to resemble a crusty old man. A typical tale from Herefordshire describes how a changeling is banished and the real child rescued by making a brew of malt and hops, stuffing it into an eggshell and cooking it over an open fire. At this sight, the changeling speaks for the first time in its life, crying: 'I am old, but I never saw a man brewing beer in an eggshell before!' It then leaps from its cradle and is chased around the room and out of the door – just as the real child returns, now grown into a healthy lad, and bringing an extraordinary account of how he was raised by the fairies under the hill. Other variants of this widely known story recommend ways of getting the real child back, such as throwing the changeling on a blazing fire so that it flies up the chimney. If the real child does not then return spontaneously, the parents might have to fetch him themselves from the fairies' hill. A Cornish variant is gentler: here a baby is taken by the fairies from its slovenly, drunken, neglectful mother and is eventually found, beautifully bathed, tended and wrapped in flowers, inspiring a great improvement in its mother's behaviour.

Adults too could be abducted – an event which seems to have been particularly common in Cornwall, where historical accounts record two young women – Anne Jefferies and Cherry of Zennor – who separately claimed to have been taken into the fairy realms. Another common tale, known in Northumberland, Yorkshire and elsewhere, is of an older woman taken 'into the hill' by a fairy man – sometimes the fairy king himself – in order to act as midwife and nurse to his wife, who is about to give birth. When the fairy baby is born, the old woman is instructed to regularly apply magic ointment to the child's eyes, but forbidden to use it herself. Eventually she breaks the taboo and puts some of the ointment into her own eye – which gives her 'fairy sight', enabling her to see enchanted scenes normally denied to ordinary mortals. In some variants, her disobedience is discovered and she is banished as a punishment; in others she manages to keep it secret and is sent home with a bag of fairy gold. At a later date the woman sees the fairies causing mischief at a fair, believing themselves to be hidden from mortal eyes; she gives herself away and is punished by being blinded in the eye to which she had applied the ointment. On the other hand, from Lancashire comes a story of more benevolent fairies, who give a similar magic ointment to a young boy to cure his failing sight.

One of the most haunting accounts of supposed encounters with fairies comes from Suffolk where, in the twelfth-century reign of King Stephen, a strange girl and boy with green skin, and speaking an alien tongue, were found in a pit. The boy would eat nothing but green beans and soon died, but his sister took more varied food, and so she thrived and lost her green colour. Eventually, she was able to tell of her country of origin, where all the people were green and lived in a kind of twilight; the children had left it by mistake, being trapped in a cavern and unable to find the correct way out.

Fairies and humans interact in many other ways. A story from Somerset tells of a farmer willing to do a fairy a favour by mending a broken stool or tool. He is rewarded with a magic cake, and after eating it his fortunes take a turn for the better. A more common gift of gratitude is a bag of fairy gold, or a set of wishes, but such offerings are often tainted by malicious trickery. A Northamptonshire woodcutter, who sees the Little People dancing in a local fairy ring, obeys an order from a disembodied voice not to cut down a particular tree. In return he is granted three wishes, but he and his wife fall into an argument and waste all the wishes on trivialities. A Lincolnshire youth rescues a strange fairy man called Yallery Brown from under a stone, and in return the little man does all his work for him. But this causes so much envy and trouble amongst the other workers that the youth is dismissed. When he begs Yallery Brown to leave him alone, he is cursed with bad luck for the rest of his life.

In other parts, it is the fairies themselves who do the good deeds for the humans. In Surrey and Worcestershire, the fairies were said to specialize in lending or mending tools for their human neighbours: all one had to do was request an item, or leave one for repair at a designated spot, and the wish would be fulfilled. A Devon story tells of the fairies helping a farmer with his threshing; he takes care to feed them and respect their privacy, and in return they top up his store with some enchanted corn of their own, enabling the farmer to sell extra and thus achieve great wealth. From Derbyshire, however, comes a story similar to the Grimm Brothers' well-known *Elves and the Shoemaker*, in which the fairies' generosity turns out to be a burden. It tells of a poor cobbler who is aided in his work by a fairy man called Hob Thrust. In the end, Hob makes so many shoes that they overflow all over the house, and the cobbler is obliged to rid himself of the flood by throwing them all from the window.

The key is not to cause offence to the fairies by prying on them: those who ignore this rule risk losing the fairies' benevolence or even worse. From Lancashire comes the tale of two villagers who chance upon a fairy funeral. When one breaks the taboo not to watch it, he recognizes one of the corpses as himself. A Shropshire story tells of a man called Wild Edric, who happens upon some fairy revels and falls in love with one of the dancers there (who in this case is of human size). After three days of his entreaties, she finally agrees to marry him – but warns him never to speak aloud of her immortal origins. They live in married bliss for many years, until in a moment of rage he blurts out the forbidden facts, causing her to vanish for ever and leaving him to die of a broken heart.

Generally, people were advised to be wary of fairies, who were characterized more by cunning than by helpfulness. A particular danger was to be struck by elf-shot from a fairy bow, which could cause an 'elf-stroke' (paralytic seizure). According to Briggs, this is the origin of the medical term 'stroke'. Any lingering or degenerative illness might be attributed to this. Fairy food was best avoided, for in many cases it would cause those who ate it to forget their normal life and thus become imprisoned in Fairyland. Another hazard was to be 'pixie-led' by the little people, thus losing one's way. In *A Dictionary of Fairies*, Briggs quotes women in Devon and Cornwall who claimed to have experienced this as recently as the 1960s. However, it was easy to take precautions against it: it was said that fairies would lose their power or flee if one carried something made of iron, or the branch of a rowan tree, a four-leafed clover, St John's wort, a daisy, salt, bread, or a sacred symbol such as a cross or prayerbook. They could be deflected by prayers or hymn-singing, and would not dare to cross either holy water or running water, so that it was possible to escape them by jumping across a stream.

The Devil's Bargain
Grice: *Folk Tales of Lancashire*

This is actually an amalgam of two stories from the same source book. The conjuring up of the Devil by some schoolboys appears in *A Legend of Burnley*; the rest of the tale can be found in *The Devil and the Schoolmaster of Cockerham*.

'Talk of the Devil,' the saying goes, 'and he's sure to appear' – and this is a recurring theme of English stories about the Devil, which form a large body of native folklore. For a being reputed to be the personification of pure evil, it is perhaps surprising how many places are named after him. However, the Devil of folklore is not as monstrous and terrifying as the medieval Church would have had its flock believe. Indeed, he comes over as a rather comical and pathetic character, a trickster who is easily outwitted, one whom everybody loves to hate and perhaps even secretly longs to encounter to prove how easy it is to get the better of him.

Although some Devil stories have tragic conclusions, the majority see him routed, with his human adversaries having the last laugh.

There are many euphemisms for the Devil: Old Nick, the Old 'Un, the Old Lad or the Old Gentleman, the Demon Huntsman, Satan or His Satanic Majesty, the Evil One, Lucifer and the Arch-Fiend. He can fly, breathe fire, cause spontaneous combustion and shape-shift. He almost always appears in disguise, but sharp-eyed victims who look downwards will realize his true identity from his cloven feet, which he often attempts to conceal in outsized boots. He materializes before those who take his name in vain, or who make rash vows such as 'I don't care if I go to Hell'; but it is just as easy to be rid of him by praying, clutching a Bible or making a statement 'in the name of the Lord'.

The Devil can turn up anywhere, sometimes even in churches – a type of building which, for obvious reasons, he despises. A number of anecdotes scattered around the country tell of his interference with the construction of churches, for example demolishing the workmen's efforts each night until they relocate the sacred building to a place that causes him less offence. The Devil's Punchbowl at Kirby Lonsdale in Cumbria is said to have a complete church buried underneath it, after the Devil dropped a rock on it. Likewise, many curious natural landscape features such as Cheddar Gorge in Somerset and Devil's Dyke in Sussex are said to have been created by him – like giants, the Devil has a penchant for digging enormous holes and trenches, and hurling boulders about.

The classic Devil story features the person who foolishly sells his soul to the Devil in return for some short-lived material gain. A Devon man does this, promising that the Devil can also have his skin when he dies, and naming a particular friend to oversee the flaying of his corpse. When he dies, the terrified friend seeks help from the parson, who advises him to keep his appointment with the Devil, but to carry a cockerel with him. Sure enough, as soon as the Devil speaks, the cockerel crows – compelling the Devil to vanish. Another Devon resident, a girl jilted by her lover in favour of another, eagerly accepts the help of a handsome youth who offers to facilitate her revenge if she will promise herself to him. In a blind rage, she allows the youth to goad her into stabbing her faithless sweetheart and his new lover; but when the deed is done, the youth resumes his true satanic form and sweeps her into an abyss with a pack of baying spectral hounds.

Irresponsible bragging, and swearing on the Devil's name, are hazardous. A boastful Herefordshire tailor is visited by the Devil, who orders him to make a suit. The tailor escapes the Evil One's clutches by refusing to accept payment, shielded by a parson who recites prayers non-stop on his behalf until cock-crow. Another tailor, this time in Northumberland, announces to a crowded inn that he can sew a coat using less cloth than anyone else – even for the Devil. He doesn't realize that the silent stranger watching him from a corner is the Evil One himself: he follows the tailor home in the dark and gives him a week to fulfil his claim, otherwise he will have him 'body and soul'. A priest advises the chastened tailor to make the coat one half full of faults and the other half perfect, so that when the Devil tries to catch him out with bad workmanship, he always has a good retort. This rather simplistic trick works, and after a lengthy argument the Devil stalks off in disgust.

In Somerset, it is a pretty young bride who conjures up the Devil by her thoughtless oath. Her wedding is being celebrated with wild dancing out of doors in a circle of standing stones, and when the pious piper packs up at midnight, the lady insists that a replacement must be found 'even if it means going to Hell to get someone'. At once a bearded old man appears, playing a tune so frenzied that all the guests are compelled to dance ever faster and faster without stopping (another parallel with fairies). By dawn, the Devil has revealed his true shape, and the dancers have all turned into skeletons.

In some stories, the Devil appears to be almost kindly. A Yorkshire cobbler on his way home through the countryside sings a jolly song about the Devil – and finds the Evil One at his side, joining in! They share jokes and an alcohol-laden picnic, and then the cobbler asks the Devil to provide proof of their meeting by building a bridge over the stream to impress his friends. Sure enough, a stone bridge miraculously appears in the very spot just three days later. A Northamptonshire boy is ordered to manure a field while the farmer is away, but he spends the allotted time in idleness, and then cries with despair at his anticipated punishment. The Devil appears and offers to do the job 'in the short time that it will take you to run to that stile and leap over it, but if I finish before you reach it, you're mine!' The boy just manages to escape in time and the farmer rewards him for the Devil's labours, but by the next day all the manuring has been undone. A Cumbrian woman finds herself stranded on the opposite side of a flooded river from her husband. The Devil appears and offers to build them a bridge, on condition that he can have the first living thing to cross it. They agree; the bridge appears in an instant and the couple save their souls by luring a dog on to the bridge before them.

Fortunately, it is virtually always possible to get rid of a demonic visitation. A Worcestershire farmer discovers too late that his super-efficient new labourer is actually the Devil. He seeks advice from a wise man, who advises him to set the Devil an impossible task, for failure will cause the Evil One to vanish. At the first few attempts, the Devil gets the better of him, but finally a gypsy woman helpfully suggests that he give the Devil a strand of his wife's curly hair and take it to be beaten straight at the blacksmith's – a truly impossible task that can never be completed. A more straightforward solution comes from Somerset. St Dunstan, an Anglo-Saxon abbot, is hammering some ornate goldwork in his solitary cell when the Devil appears before him, tempting him in the shape of a voluptuous young girl. The celibate monk has no interest in her enticing words, recognizes her as the Evil One – and gives her a nasty nip on the nose with his white-hot tongs!

The Princess and the Fool

Briggs: *A Dictionary of British Folk-Tales*

This story belongs to the genre of nonsense tales, which is very popular in English tradition. It gives another fine example of the 'Jack' character who, despite the most unpromising beginnings, ends up triumphant.

There is another humorous story about a feisty Canterbury woman called *The Bewitched Tree*. The heroine of this rather bawdy tale is a commoner, already married but discontented with her elderly husband and eager to have 'a bit on the side' with their manservant. The servant contrives a trick that will enable them to make love right before her husband's eyes without punishment. The three protagonists go walking in the garden and the woman asks the servant to fetch her an apple from a tall tree. He climbs into the highest branches, looks down and cries out to his master in mock outrage: 'Sir, I can see you down there getting intimate with your wife – that is most unseemly in a public place!' The embarrassed husband strongly denies this, to which the servant replies that the tree must be bewitched, causing those who climb it to have visions. Of course the master disbelieves him, so the servant suggests they swap places so that the master can experience the strange effect for himself. The sceptical master climbs the tree while the servant seizes the chance to cuckold him. The master clearly sees them at it, but supposes it is indeed a mere hallucination induced by the magic tree!

A favourite form of nonsense tale involves mocking the inhabitants of a particular village, who are supposedly simpletons. Briggs says that over fifty locations are traditionally lampooned in this way, including five villages in Wiltshire, six in Yorkshire, and three each in Oxfordshire and Staffordshire. The best-known collections of these witty anecdotes tell of *The Wise Men of Gotham* in Nottinghamshire. They record the foolish inhabitants trying to do the following: imprison a cuckoo in a hedge in the hope that it will sing all year; put salted fish into a pond to breed, then attempt to drown the eel that eats them; send a cheese to market 'all by itself' by rolling it downhill; search for a needle in a field of newly sewn grass, and carry bales of corn to market on their own backs to spare their horses the burden. Meanwhile, at Coggeshall in Essex, the simple folk light a fire under a plum tree to hasten the fruit into ripening. These villagers also decide there is not enough wind to turn two windmills and so cut one of them down, and when a rabid dog bites a wheelbarrow, they chain the barrow inside a shed in case it should go mad. In Ebrington and Ilminton, two Warwickshire villages, the inhabitants put their clocks forward to make Christmas come sooner, and when they buy a new wheelbarrow, they carry it around so that its wheels won't bruise the ground. The people of Lorbottle, Northumberland, are famed for trying to pick up the moon like a round of cheese in the hope of hanging it in the trees to shine every night; however, they never manage to get hold of it, as it is always hiding behind the next hill. These stories seem touched with a particularly English sense of humour, yet similar ones have also been collected in many European countries as well as Africa, India and the Philippines.

A more developed form of nonsense tale is known as *The Three Sillies*, again with versions told in many counties. In the Shropshire version, a girl is drawing beer from the cellar for her sweetheart, when she suddenly bursts into tears. Her parents enquire about the cause of her anguish and she tells them: 'I was just imagining that I married my sweetheart and we had a son and when he was old enough, he came down here to fetch some beer like I'm doing now, and there was a mallet up on the shelf there and it fell on his head – wouldn't that be terrible!' At this, the mother and father become distraught too, and the bemused sweetheart declares he has never heard such nonsense, but if he can find three other people as silly as them, he will hasten back to marry the girl. He wanders through the world and soon comes to a woman living in a turf-roofed house, who refuses to cut the grass growing on the roof and throw it down to her cow. Instead she insists on trying to drag the cow up on to the roof to eat it. Next, staying at an inn, he shares a room with a man who can't put on his trousers because he has rigged them up on a contraption of poles and is trying to jump into them. Finally, he sees a whole group of people trying to rake the moon's reflection out of a pond. At this, he returns home to marry the girl. An Essex variant says the foolish heroine starts crying because, instead of doing the cooking that her mother has set her, she worries that a brick will fall down the chimney on to her head as she leans over the fire. Her bemused sweetheart misses out on the 'moon-raking' experience, but finds a woman trying to haul an oven to her tin of dough so she can bake it, instead of taking the dough to the oven. In Oxfordshire, the tearful heroine is called Thoughtful Moll and her sweetheart, Dob, observes a woman trying to catch sunshine in a hat so she can use it to dry her rain-soaked corn. In Devon, Mary Jane worries that she will have a son who will fall into a well and drown; the silly sights seen by her sweetheart, Tom, include a boy trying to feed his hens boiling water in the hope that they will lay boiled eggs!

Another stylized form within the genre focuses on particular characters – sometimes real people, sometimes imaginary. In the Black Country of the Midlands there is a whole set of stories about two friends called Enoch and Eli. The stories appear to be fairly modern in provenance, for some refer to factories, council houses and pubs, though others are more timeless. Enoch appears in the pub and Eli remarks that he is wearing odd shoes. 'I know,' says Enoch, 'I've another pair like them at home.' When Enoch moves house, his new neighbour's chickens keep him awake at night; his solution is to buy the chickens off him, so he can keep his neighbour awake instead. In Cambridge, a host of tall tales has grown up around Pal Hall, a real builder who lived in the city in the late nineteenth century. Once, he built a privy in his garden and forgot to include a door so he found himself walled up inside.

There are also many one-off jests. A man from Burton-on-Trent buys a live eel and keeps it in his wife's washtub, but on washday he transfers it to his own pocket and takes it to the pub, where it develops a taste for beer. Eventually, the eel finds its own way to the pub where it runs up a huge debt. In an unnamed Somerset village, the people want to make their little church as fine as the one in the neighbouring village, so they put earth around it to help it grow. In Sussex, the yokels are contemptuous of a Cockney visitor who acts as if he is superior to them, so they invite him to go owl-catching. They send him into a barn with a sieve to catch the owls in, but the barn is booby-trapped with buckets of water in the rafters, so he is drenched.

These stories all contain the roots of the brash humour of the comic book and music hall. They hark back to more innocent, self-disparaging times and are very much part of the heritage of 'the common people'.

The Seventh Swan

Tongue: *Forgotten Folktales of the English Counties*

The source book says that the story was collected as recently as 1963, at a meeting of the Women's Institute.

The act of changing shape between human and animal or inanimate form is common in the myths and fairy tales of virtually all cultures, and takes two different forms.

A shape-shifter is a person or animal with the inbuilt ability to change shape spontaneously – either on demand, or when particular circumstances occur. In British folklore, this is a common characteristic both of witches, who often appear as hares, and fairies. Other examples are werewolves, who turn into their animal form at certain phases of the moon, and the Greek god Zeus, who variously assumes the shape of a swan, a bull and even a shower of gold in order to seduce mortal maidens. Many shape-shifters are tricksters, like Anansi, an Afro-Caribbean who changes wilfully between the form of a spider and an old man; others are semi-divine, such as the Chinese dragon-princesses who leave their human forms by swallowing a magic pearl. The most famous shape-shifter in English traditional stories is Morgan le Fay, the wicked half-sister of King Arthur, who turns herself into a deer in order to lure Arthur deep into the forest and steal his magic scabbard. She later becomes an adder, whose presence ends the truce between Arthur and his arch-enemy, causing the king's last battle and his fatal wounding.

Transformation, on the other hand, occurs when a person is *forced* to change shape by the malevolent spells of a witch or magician – often to avenge an imagined insult or a broken taboo. The spell may be broken by a magic object, or the demonstration of selfless 'true love' by a third party – exactly as in *King Arthur and the Hideous Hag*.

The 'swan maiden' story is a variant of the shape-changing theme and is known throughout Europe, the Middle East, Asia, Australasia, East Africa and South America. The usual plot is that a young man chances on a flock of swans (or some other bird – in South America it may be a parrot or vulture) landing on a lake. Here the birds shed their feathers and instantly change into beautiful maidens. He falls in love with one and hides her feathers so that, when her companions turn back into swans to fly away, she is unable to join them. He approaches the distressed maiden, treats her kindly, persuades her to marry him and, usually, they have children. But she always remains restless and eventually retrieves her feathers, resumes her swan shape and flies away, never to return.

A variant in *The Arabian Nights* sees the abandoned husband follow her on an astonishing supernatural adventure back to her land of origin, where he rescues her from a mortal punishment inflicted by her fearsome father and eventually brings her and their children home to live happily ever after. Similarly, in an Irish myth, the princess Caer Ibormeith is transformed into a swan by her jealous father on alternate years, in order to prevent her from marrying; she is finally rescued by the god of love, Oenghus, who turns himself into a swan too and carries her away to his enchanted realm. However, these are rare exceptions to the usually tragic ending. A well-known Scottish variant is the 'selkie' story, in which the maidens shape-shift into seals, but the story form and outcome follow the usual haunting and melancholy pattern. For most of the old storytellers agreed that marriage between a mortal and immortal was almost inevitably doomed to failure.

The Knight of York

Gee: *Folk Tales of Yorkshire*
Jacobs: *English Fairy Tales*

This belongs to the genre of 'rags to riches' or 'Cinderella' stories – one of the most popular types of fairy tale in the world: indeed there are said to be over 500 versions in Europe alone. The motif is known as far afield as the Middle East, China, Native America and West Africa. Even within the British Isles there are a number of variants.

The classic plot proceeds as follows. A helpless ash-girl (so called because of her humble status in tending the household fire) or goose-girl is rejected by some or all of her family, but aided by a benevolent magic helper. A grand feast or ball is held and, although the girl is too lowly to be invited, the magic helper disguises her as a wealthy lady and enables her to attend. (In some versions, she attends on three separate occasions: the 'power of three' is a common motif in traditional stories all over the world.) At the event a nobleman falls in love with her, but before he can propose, she is compelled to vanish by a special deadline. The love-struck nobleman searches for her far and wide, often setting a special test by which to identify her; he finds her, she passes the test, and they marry and live happily ever after, sometimes seeing the family member(s) who rejected her justly punished.

Though *Cinderella* is known and loved by even the youngest children in this country, the story is not home-grown. It was first written down in 1697 in a little book called *Stories, or Tales from Times Past, with Morals* (subtitled *Tales of Mother Goose*) by a Frenchman, Charles Perrault, in a style that surely reflected the grandeur of the pre-revolutionary French court. Here the magic helper is a fairy godmother, but in other versions it may be a supernatural animal, or even the girl's dead mother, for the loss of a natural parent and persecution by a cruel stepmother is a familiar theme. In Perrault, the lovesick prince finds her because she is the only lady in the land who can fit into a single glass slipper (left behind when she fled the ball). However, in *The Knight of York* and some other English forms, she is identified by a special ring.

Catskin is a parallel English tale which, according to Jacobs, exists in seventy-three different versions. Here, the heroine is rejected by her rich father, who regrets that she is not a son, and at fifteen she is ordered to marry a 'nasty, rough old man'. She seeks help from a hen-wife who, although unskilled in magic, is able to give her some suitably mysterious advice. She tells the girl to reject her hateful suitor unless she is given a coat of silver cloth. The request is met, and following the hen-wife's advice, she next demands a coat of beaten gold, then one made from 'the feathers of all the birds of the air', and finally one made of cats' skins. Dressed in the 'catskin', she poses as a pauper and obtains work in a castle scullery. Soon the young lord of the castle holds a ball, which she attends incognito, disguised in her silver coat. He falls in love with her, but she flees. She attends two further balls in her other special coats, and when she runs from the last one, the lord follows her and discovers that she is really his catskin-clad scullery maid. His mother tries to stop him marrying her, but gives in when doctors warn that he will die if he and the girl do not marry. They live happily ever after, and she is even reconciled with her father.

The theme of a girl defined by her idiosyncratic garments is repeated in a Lincolnshire story, *Tattercoats*. The heroine is rejected by her grandfather because her mother (his daughter) died giving birth to her. He makes her wear rags as she grows up, hence she gains the nickname of Tattercoats. When the grandfather is invited to the royal ball where a bride will be chosen for the prince, he refuses to take Tattercoats, but luckily she has a true friend in the form of a young gooseherd, who takes her to town to watch the guests arriving. On their way, they encounter a stranger who asks them for directions to the palace. He sees Tattercoats dancing to the gooseherd's pipe and falls in love with her. He persuades them both to come to the palace at midnight to repeat the performance, and as she dances there, her ragged clothes are transformed into a fine dress. The stranger now reveals that he is really the prince, and claims the girl as his bride, with the usual happy ending. The gooseherd, having completed his subtly magic role, now vanishes, and the cruel grandfather is left alone to wallow in his ill temper.

In a Suffolk story, *Cap o' Rushes*, a rich man asks his three daughters to declare the depths of their affection for him, and then banishes the youngest for the insult of saying that she loves him 'as much as salt'. Clad in a cloak made of rushes, she finds work as a kitchen maid at a grand house. Here, a series of three balls are held, which she attends disguised in finery from her former life, vanishing at the end to return to the kitchen. As in other stories, the master's son falls in love with her, and begins to pine away when he cannot trace her. In her guise as a maid, Cap o' Rushes brings him a bowl of gruel in which she has secretly hidden a ring. Through this he joyfully identifies her and their wedding is arranged. Cap o' Rushes invites her father to the feast, but orders all the dishes to be left unsalted, rendering them inedible. Thus the old man realizes that salt is one of the most valuable things in the world, and the pair are reconciled. This is surely one of the stories that inspired Shakespeare's *King Lear*.

All the stories so far cited see a heroine rejected by either a father or grandfather, but two other English tales take up the more familiar 'Cinderella' theme of a wicked stepmother. In *The Three Heads of the Well*, the widowed King of Colchester (Essex) marries again, bringing his daughter a stepmother and a stepsister who despise her and turn the king against her. Eventually, the unloved princess leaves home and wanders aimlessly through the world until she meets an old man by a cave. She shares her meagre ration of food with him, and in return he gives her a wand that allows her to break through an enchanted hedge. On the other side she finds a well, from which three golden heads emerge and beg her to wash and comb them, which she does. In return they gift her with extra beauty and good fortune, and before long she is married to another, mightier king. When her stepsister hears of this, she tries to emulate the adventure, but because she refuses to help both the old man and the three golden heads, she is cursed into poverty, and the wicked stepmother hangs herself in disgust. This story omits the 'incognito attendance at a ball' motif, but contains another very widespread theme in folk tales: kindness rewarded and wickedness punished. The old man is clearly cast as a magic helper, though he is somewhat overshadowed by the three mysterious golden heads.

The Rose Tree, another Lincolnshire story, is only loosely linked to the theme of rags to riches, but it is of interest here for its continuation of the 'wicked stepmother' motif. A widower has a daughter by his first wife and a son by his second. The second wife, hating her beautiful stepdaughter, pretends to comb her hair but instead cuts off her head. She then serves the girl's heart and liver to her unsuspecting father. The girl is buried underneath a rose tree, where a white bird sits singing the story of her murder. Eventually, the bird rattles a millstone against the roof of the house, and when the stepmother runs out to investigate the noise, it drops the stone on her head and kills her.

All these stories share a focus: a child's dread of rejection by her parents – but also the *necessity* of some kind of rejection if she is to become a fully independent adult and make her own way in the world. However, the best-known English rags-to-riches story, *Dick Whittington*, takes quite a different form, featuring a boy as its main protagonist. It is a more worldly and straightforward tale of 'luck' rather than an exploration of family relationships or emotional development. Dick is an orphan and beggar, who goes to London believing that its streets are paved with gold. He is given employment by a rich merchant and buys a cat because the garret where he sleeps is overrun by rats and mice. He is persuaded to send the cat away as an 'investment' on one of the merchant's ships, but misses it badly and intends to return home. However, the sound of Bow Bells seemingly ringing out 'Turn again Whittington, Lord Mayor of London' persuades him to stay. Meanwhile, his cat has arrived at the Barbary Coast, where it rids the Moorish king and queen of a terrible plague of rats, a service for which Dick is paid a huge fortune. Now extremely rich, Dick marries the merchant's daughter and fulfils the bells' prophesy. Jacobs says that the real Richard Whittington was Lord Mayor of London in 1397, 1406 and 1419.

The Wicked Witch

Jacobs: *English Fairy Tales*

In Jacobs's version, the heroine is actually one of two sisters. After the heroine has returned home, the witch escapes from the oven and the second sister sets out to repeat the adventure, hoping also to make her fortune. She declines to help the three bewitched creatures, so that when she runs off with the treasure, they fail to help her in return, enabling the witch to catch and beat her.

Wicked witches are a staple of children's fairy tales. However, in English storytelling tradition there are few such deliciously unambiguous villainesses, for most witch tales fall more correctly into the category of 'historical anecdote'. Rather than being harmless fantasy, they reflect the fear, in earlier times, of any unconventional woman and must be seen against the unsavoury practice of witch-hunts. There are countless tales of 'weird women' who had supposedly sold their souls to the Devil, many ending in the accused woman's violent death. Such witches were blamed for many common or garden ills – sickness of people or livestock, premature death, even the inability of a dairymaid to make butter.

It was claimed that many of these witches could shape-shift, particularly into the form of a hare, and that such animals were easy to recognize as witches since they could always escape any marksman. Others might turn into cats, toads, hedgehogs or even elder trees, often of supernatural proportions and moving at prodigious speed. A Devon witch was notorious for raising a magic mist and luring people into a 'quaking bog'. In Leicestershire, a cave-dwelling witch known as Black Annis supposedly snatched people from their cottages, clawed them to death, sucked out their blood and then hung up their skins to dry. Another cannibalistic witch lived in Lincolnshire.

It was difficult, but not impossible, to get the better of such hags: the key was to work one's own counter-magic. A Lancashire farmer, who claimed his cattle, crops and even children were blighted by witches, got rid of them by carrying a candle around the witches' meeting place on Hallowe'en night; the following year his luck turned and he became quite prosperous. A Nottinghamshire carter found his horses paralysed after he refused to share his tobacco with a known witch: the cure was to scratch her arm with a needle, and as soon as her blood began to flow, the horses could move again. Another carter, in Worcestershire, believed the cat causing havoc in his stable to be a witch: his hunch was proved correct when his dog tried to chase it away and it transformed into a wheat straw, which oozed blood when the carter cut through it with a knife. A Yorkshire man succeeded in shooting a 'witch-hare' by using shot made from Communion silverware, which had been melted down in an iron ladle and smeared with hare's blood. In such instances, when an animal suspected of being a witch was destroyed, it could usually be linked with the sudden illness or death of a local woman accused of dabbling in the dark arts.

Only occasionally would humour creep into these witch tales – as in the one about a Shropshire woman who was carrying a bag of flour home and met a witch on the way. 'That's not flour,' said the witch, 'it's manure.' And sure enough, when the woman looked, it was. But when she returned home and told the sorry tale to her husband, it had turned into flour again.

There were also stories of 'good' witches. One of them, who lived in Somerset, successfully told a cottager how to cure his bewitched pig by letting its blood onto a rag, then burning the rag behind locked doors while he read aloud from the Bible. Another witch from the same county could heal sick people and was a skilled prophetess. She correctly predicted that treasure would be found when water pipes were laid across a particular coomb (short valley or deep hollow). However, it was dangerous to offend her, as a shopkeeper found to his cost when he nagged her to settle his account, and found a rat haunting his bedroom. Occasionally, these benevolent witches were men, such as Wrightson, the 'wise man' of Stokeley in Yorkshire, whose powers were derived from being the seventh son of a seventh daughter; or the Wizard of Lincoln, who could transform himself into a blackbird and enable victims of crime to identify the culprits by casting their shadows on a wall.

The most famous of all English witches was Mother Shipton of Yorkshire, supposedly the daughter of a woman and the Devil. Probably a real person and respectably married, she seems to have been physically deformed, with an astonishing intellect and charismatic powers. According to the stories that sprang up around her, she predicted many modern inventions including cars, broadcasting and submarines. She was also notorious for casting mischievous spells, such as spoiling a party by making all the guests laugh without being able to cease; when they fled, invisible hands pelted them with flying apples, and ugly she-imps clung to their horses all the way home. Mother Shipton was eventually hauled up before the judges, but succeeded in escaping and vanishing, mounted upon a winged dragon.

A more truly fantastical tale from an old ballad tells of the infamous Alison Gross, 'the ugliest witch in the north country', who failed to seduce a young man and so took revenge by transforming him into a 'worm' – a dragon or snake. His distraught sister went to the forest to tend him every Saturday night until Hallowe'en, when the fairy queen came riding past and broke the witch's spell by taking the worm on to her knee and stroking it three times until it turned back into its true form.

The Asrai

Briggs: *A Dictionary of British Folk-Tales*

This story is actually a combination of two related Shropshire anecdotes. The asrai are inland water fairies, closely related to mermaids (for in European tradition these beautiful women with fishtails could swim from the sea upstream into fresh water). The ancestors of the asrai in this story must have travelled some distance, for there is no coast in Shropshire. River mermaids also lived in neighbouring Herefordshire, for it is recorded that when the bell of Marden Church fell into the river, it was snatched by a mermaid who refused to let men or horses take it away. Eventually, a wise man recommended that it could be dragged from the water while the mermaid was asleep inside it, by using a team of twelve heifers with yew-wood yokes and rowan-wood bands. But one of the drivers broke the silence which was essential while the task was carried out, waking the mermaid who carried the bell back to the riverbed. There it is still said to lie.

Although England has an extensive coastline, it has far fewer mermaid tales than Wales or Scotland. The two most memorable ones come from Cornwall. *The Old Man of Cury* tells of an old fisherman who sees a mermaid sitting on a rock near Kynance Cove at low tide. She is cut off from the sea by a long stretch of sand, and the old man honours her request for him to carry her back to the waves where her husband is waiting for her. In return, she offers him any reward he chooses. He declines money but asks for the power of healing and breaking spells, to which the mermaid readily agrees. She gives him the comb from her hair and tells him to stroke the sea with it whenever he desires to speak to her. Over the years, he does this many times and she grants his wish, giving him supernatural powers that pass through his family for generations. This form of plot is shared by mermaid tales all over Europe.

Lutey and the Mermaid starts off in the same way, but has an unfortunate ending. As the fisherman carries the mermaid back to the water, she clings to him and tries to enchant him into following her under the waves. Luckily, his dog starts barking, breaking the spell, and he threatens to stab the mermaid to death unless she releases him. She swims out to sea, but nine years later she keeps her promise to return and bewitches him to plunge into the water beside her. He is never seen again, and every nine years after that, one of his relations is drowned at sea.

The ending of the latter story is in keeping with dominant mermaid beliefs, for the creatures were widely dreaded as harbingers of ill luck.

Like fairies, mermaids could be generous to mortals whom they liked or who had helped them, but they were also fickle and it was dangerous to offend them. A tale from Staithes, North Yorkshire, tells of two mermaids washed up on the beach after a storm, only to be incarcerated, mocked and even stoned by the locals. When they finally escape, they curse the village, and as a result part of it is lost to floods.

A mermaid's appearance – often singing with haunting sweetness as she perches upon a rock – might herald a violent storm or some other disaster. Even worse, she might lure sailors to drown in the waters beside her. Escape was only possible for those with a strong will. A Norfolk story tells of trawlermen who are fishing from two separate boats off the coast of Scotland; a mermaid with long green hair comes drifting past them on a wrecked ship. The men on one boat avert their eyes, clutch their knives (for iron is believed to be effective against all kinds of enchantment and malevolent beings) and manage to survive, but the men on the other boat are transfixed by her until she capsizes their boat and sees them all drowned.

There appear to be no English stories about mortals marrying mermaids, although these were well known in other parts of the British Isles. Perhaps that is just as well, for the descendants of such unions were often cursed by dumbness or the inability to sleep. However, a story from Somerset tells of a fisherman who adopts a stranded sea morgan (a Celtic term for a mermaid) baby, but after only a short time it is frightened back into the waves by his interfering neighbours.

The Forbidden Forest

Tongue: *Forgotten Folktales of the English Counties*

The theme of an evil king taking a new wife every night and killing her once he has satisfied his lust is clearly inspired by the frame story of *The Arabian Nights*.

The whole forest in this tale seems to be enchanted, and similar supernatural places feature in the traditional stories of many countries, where they may be reached by climbing a magic tree or ladder into the sky, or diving into water. However, the enchanted realms of England are all firmly earthbound.

The best known is Fairyland, which the chosen may enter through a tunnel, a tangle of thorns or a stone door in the hills. A seventeenth-century Cornish girl called Anne Jefferies claimed to have been taken there by a group of miniscule fairies who actually carried her through the air. She described Fairyland as very beautiful, and full of temples, palaces, flowers, fruit trees and lakes, all lavishly decorated with gold and silver. When she returned, she developed powers as a clairvoyant and healer, even though sceptics claimed her experience was merely a vision resulting from a fit. There are many stories from all over Britain of older women abducted into Fairyland in order to act as midwife and nurse to a fairy queen. Some perceive it as a gloomy place of damp, cobweb-infested caves; only those who manage to apply magic ointment to their eyes see it in its true magnificence.

England's other famous enchanted place is Avalon, sometimes known as the Isle of Apples, which is strongly linked to Arthurian legend. It was here that King Arthur's magic sword, Excalibur, was forged by fairy smiths. Avalon was also the site where the king was taken to be healed when he was mortally wounded in his final battle. There seem to be no records of any ordinary people going there. Tradition has it that Arthur reached the isle by crossing a great lake in a mystical boat, in which he was nursed by nine dark queens as it drifted through the mist.

A Derbyshire folk tale tells of an enchanted world under the ground, strongly linked to the mining industry. The three sons of a lead-miner set out separately to seek their fortunes. Each one encounters a 'little, red, hairy man' who asks him to share his food. The two eldest refuse him and are punished by returning home empty-handed, but the youngest son shares his rations generously. The little man rewards him by taking him down an old mine shaft into a parallel world where he rescues three princesses from giants living in three castles made respectively of copper, silver and gold. He marries the golden princess and returns home to build himself a mansion. But when his brothers try to emulate him and find the enchanted world for themselves, the shaft rope breaks, the mine collapses and they are buried within it.

In a Lancashire story, a fisherman drifting in his boat in the bay at night hears bells ringing under the sea and falls into a trance. He awakens in a strange seascape under a coloured moon, where the boat moves of its own accord. He lands in a country of 'little folk' who spend all day at their revels and grant every wish. However, when he unintentionally offends their queen by kissing her foot, her soldiers beat him severely and he eventually wakes up in his own boat.

A common aspect of visits to such places is the strange way that time passes there. The spending of many years in an enchanted land may be equivalent to just a few minutes of time in the real world, or vice versa. Some visitors to such places may be unable to escape until long past the end of their natural lifespan, so that when they return to the real world, they crumble into dust. Such catastrophes are most likely to happen to those who partake of food or drink there, for to do so is usually taboo.

The role of trees in this story is deeply rooted in English folklore. In ancient times, oaks were considered sacred and it was said to be dangerous to cut one down, for when coppiced shoots grew from the stump they would be filled with malice and liable to play vengeful tricks on anyone foolish enough to pass by at night. Willows could actually uproot themselves on dark nights and follow travellers, muttering eerily to themselves. These two beliefs clearly influenced Tolkien when he created the Ents, the Old Forest, Mirkwood and Lothlorien for *The Lord of the Rings*. Hawthorns – especially solitary ones – were haunted by fairies, whilst in Oxfordshire and the Midlands, elders were supposed to be transformations of witches. Some protection from dangerous spirits could be attained by sheltering under an ash or, better still, a rowan; but those who dozed off under a grafted apple tree risked being carried away by fairies. A Cumbrian tale tells of how a vixen fleeing the hounds begs the forest trees for help. The holly refuses, but a hawthorn directs her to a hideout, and she is finally sheltered inside an oak tree, which is the 'guardian of all the forest beasts'.

The King of England's Three Sons
Jacobs: *More English Fairy Tales*

This slightly tongue-in-cheek extravaganza takes the form of a quest – one of the grand themes of traditional stories worldwide – though, surprisingly, not a very common one in England. Characters who embark on a quest may be of noble or humble birth, male or female, but their adventures always follow a similar pattern. They must either achieve some impossible task (or series of tasks), or fetch back an extraordinary object from a location that is supposedly impossible to reach. To achieve this, they must overcome a series of apparently insurmountable obstacles.

Often, two or three siblings in turn set out to attempt the quest. Their fitness to complete it may be tested by one or more magic helpers – in this case, the three hideously deformed old men. Usually, the elder siblings respond to the tester's strange requests with arrogance and callousness, for which they are punished by failure to complete the mission. However, the youngest and seemingly weakest proves to be more generous or courageous than the others, and is therefore rewarded with wise advice and perhaps a magic object to help along the way. Sometimes the quest may actually be a whole series of mini-quests, each one linked: the quester may be diverted on the main journey to fulfil a task without which the larger task cannot be completed; or he succeeds in the task he has been set, but the person who has sent him on the quest is reluctant to give the promised reward, so orders yet another trial to be completed in the hope that this one will result in failure.

King Arthur and the Hideous Hag belongs partly to the quest genre, and the most famous English quest story is the grand Arthurian romance, *The Quest of the Holy Grail* (which is based on a twelfth-century Old French romance). The Grail is the dish or cup from which Christ drank at the Last Supper, and which is supposed to hold sacred drops of his blood. It appears in a vision shared by King Arthur and all his knights as they sit at the Round Table. It is said to have miraculous healing powers, and is kept in the Castle of Carbonek, in a city of the same name, but no one knows where this place lies. As soon as they see the vision, all the knights resolve to go on a quest to find the Grail. Although Arthur has forebodings that his kingdom will be weakened by their absence, he reluctantly allows them to go, knowing that if they are successful in bringing the Grail back, this will further enhance his glorious reputation.

The knights set out separately or in pairs, but although they have some interesting adventures, most meet only failure. Sir Lancelot (the king's favourite, who, unbeknown to Arthur, is having an affair with Queen Guinevere) actually manages to glimpse the Grail, but before he can reach it, he is struck by a bolt of lightning as a punishment for his adultery.

After many years, Sir Bors, Sir Perceval and Sir Galahad meet up and sail across the sea to fabled Carbonek, where they manage at last to collect the Grail. It is even more wonderful than they had imagined, and as they travel back with it, Sir Galahad absorbs its power to perform many wonderful miracles. However, they are not permitted to bring the Grail back to Arthur's kingdom, which is too full of sinners, and it passes into the permanent keeping of the legendary Fisher King.

The story is full of medieval Christian symbolism and has become a familiar metaphor for a glorious yet always unfulfilled challenge. Its unsatisfactory ending is quite different from the quests of fairy tale, which always conclude happily.

Complete List of Sources and Works Consulted

Alexander, Marc. *British Folklore, Myths and Legends* (London: Weidenfeld & Nicolson, 1982).

The Sutton Companion to British Folklore, Myths and Legends (Stroud, Gloucestershire: Sutton Publishing, 2002).

Armistead, Wilson. *Tales and Legends of the English Lakes* (London: Simpkin, Marshall & Co.; Glasgow: Thomas D. Morrison, 1891).

Briggs, Katherine M. *A Dictionary of British Folk-Tales in the English Language* incorporating the F. J. Norton Collection, (London and New York: Routledge, 1970, 1971).

A Dictionary of Fairies (London: Penguin Books, 1977).

Chaucer, Geoffrey. *The Canterbury Tales*, translated into modern English by Nevill Coghill (London: Penguin Books, 1951).

Crossley-Holland, Kevin. *Folk Tales of the British Isles* (London: Faber and Faber, 1986).

The Old Stories: Folk Tales from East Anglia and the Fen Country (London: Orion, 1999).

Dobson, R. B. and J. Taylor. *Rymes of Robyn Hood* (London: William Heinemann, 1976).

Findler, Gerald. *Legends of the Lake Counties* (Clapham via Lancaster: Dalesman Publishing Company, 1967).

Foss, Michael. *Folk Tales of the British Isles* (London: Macmillan, 1977).

Gee, H. L. *Folk Tales of Yorkshire* (London and Edinburgh: Thomas Nelson, 1952).

Grice, Frederick. *Folk Tales of the North Country* (London and Edinburgh: Thomas Nelson, 1944).
    Folk Tales of the West Midlands (London and Edinburgh: Thomas Nelson, 1952).
    Folk Tales of Lancashire (London and Edinburgh: Thomas Nelson, 1953).

Henderson, William. *Notes on the Folk-Lore of the Northern Counties of England and the Borders*, *with an Appendix of Household Stories by S. Baring-Gould* (1866; reproduced by EP Publishing, 1973).

Holt, J. C. *Robin Hood* (London: Thames & Hudson, 1983).

Hunt, Robert. *Cornish Folk-Lore* (Truro, Tor Mark Press, undated).

Jacobs, Joseph. *English Fairy Tales*, being the two collections *English Fairy Tales* and *More English Fairy Tales* (London: The Bodley Head, 1968).

Keightley, Thomas. *The Fairy Mythology* (London: G. Bell, 1878).

Killip, Kathleen. *Saint Bridget's Night: Stories from the Isle of Man* (London: Hamish Hamilton, 1975).

Lacy, Norris J. (ed.) *The Arthurian Encyclopedia* (Suffolk: The Boydell Press, 1986).

Lang, Andrew. *Blue Fairy Book* (London: Longmans, Green Co. Ltd., 1889).

Leach, Maria. *Funk & Wagnall's Standard Dictionary of Folklore, Mythology and Legend* (San Francisco: Harper & Row, 1972).

Leighton, Alexander (ed.) *Wilson's Tales of the Borders and of Scotland, Historical, Traditionary and Imaginative* (Manchester: James Ainsworth, undated, probably c.1840).

Mannheim, Ralph. *The Penguin Complete Grimms' Tales for Young and Old* (London: Penguin Books, 1984).

Quayle, Eric. *The Magic Ointment and Other Cornish Legends* (London: Andersen Press, 1986).

Riches, Samantha. *St George – Hero, Martyr and Myth* (London: Sutton Publishing, 2000).

Service, James. *Metrical Legends of Northumberland* (Alnwick: W. Davison, 1834).

Sharman, V. Day. *Folk Tales of Devon* (London and Edinburgh: Thomas Nelson, 1952).

Skinner, A. G. *Tales of the Tors* (London: The Epworth Press, 1939).

Swift, Eric. *Folk Tales of the East Midlands* (London and Edinburgh: Thomas Nelson, 1954).

Tongue, Ruth L. ***Forgotten Folktales of the English Counties*** (London: Routledge & Kegan Paul, 1970).

Walker, Peter N. ***Folk Tales from the North York Moors*** (London: Robert Hale, 1990).

Folk Stories from the Lake District (London: Robert Hale, 1993).

White, Richard (ed.) ***King Arthur in Legend and History*** (London: Dent, 1997).

Folklore, Myths and Legends of Britain (London: Reader's Digest Association, 1973).

Websites

www.mothershiptonscave.com

www.england-in-particular.com

Picture Credits

Mary Evans Picture Library/ARTHUR RACKHAM: pages 8, 13, 16, 20, 24, 30, 36, 44, 48, 70, 75, 78, 83, 86, 102, 110, 115, 121, 122, 124, 128, 130, 140

Mary Evans Picture Library: pages 41, 58, 66, 94, 98, 100–101, 118,

Other books of traditional stories by Rosalind Kerven:

The Secret World of Magic
Northumberland Folk Tales
The Fairy Spotter's Handbook
The Enchanted Forest
King Arthur
Aladdin and Other Tales from the Arabian Nights
The Giant King (Norse)
Enchanted Kingdoms (Celtic)
The Mythical Quest
Coyote Girl
Volcano Woman
The Weather Drum
The Rain Forest Story Book
In the Court of the Jade Emperor: Stories from Old China
The Woman who went to Fairyland
Earth Magic, Sky Magic: Native American Stories
King Leopard's Gift
The Tree in the Moon
The Slaying of the Dragon: Tales of the Hindu Gods
Legends of the Animal World